TIMEF HORSES TO FOLLOW

2015/16 JUMPS SEASON

CONTENTS

1	**FIFTY TO FOLLOW 2015/16**	**3**
2	**HORSES TO FOLLOW FROM IRELAND**	**49**
3	**LOOKING AHEAD**	**59**
	Talking To The Trainers	60
	Rising Stars	66
	Ante-Post Betting	71
	What's The Point?	78
4	**REVIEW OF 2014/15**	**81**
	Timeform's View On The Big Races	82
	Timeform's Best Of 2014/15	107
	2014/15 Statistics	114
5	**REFERENCE & INDEX**	**115**
	The Timeform Top 100	116
	Promising Horses	118
	Trainers For Courses	120
	Index	135

TIMEFORM

© **TIMEFORM LIMITED 2015**
COPYRIGHT AND LIABILITY

Copyright in all Timeform Publications is strictly reserved by the Publishers and no material therein may be reproduced stored in a retrieval system or transmitted in any form or by any means electronic mechanical photocopying recording or otherwise without written permission of Timeform Limited.

Timeform Horses To Follow is published by Timeform Limited, Halifax, West Yorkshire HX1 1XF (Tel: 01422 330330 Fax: 01422 398017; e-mail: timeform@timeform.com). It is supplied to the purchaser for his personal use and on the understanding that its contents are not disclosed. Except where the purchaser is dealing as a consumer (as defined in the Unfair Contract Terms Act 1977 Section 12) all conditions warranties or terms relating to fitness for purpose merchantability or condition of the goods and whether implied by Statute Common Law or otherwise are excluded and no responsibility is accepted by the Publishers for any loss whatsoever caused by any acts errors or omissions whether negligent or otherwise of the Publishers their Servants Agents or otherwise.

ISBN 978-0-9933900-0-5   Price £9.95

Printed and bound by
Charlesworth Press,
Wakefield, UK 01924 204830

TIMEFORM'S FIFTY TO FOLLOW 2015/16

SECTION 1

Timeform's Fifty To Follow, carefully chosen by members of Timeform's editorial staff, are listed below with their respective page numbers. A selection of ten (**marked in bold with a ★**) is made for those who prefer a smaller list.

A GOOD SKIN (IRE)	4	LESSONS IN MILAN (IRE)	26
AMIDON (FR)	5	MICK JAZZ (FR)	27
AUX PTITS SOINS (FR) ★	6	**MINELLA ROCCO (IRE) ★**	28
BITOFAPUZZLE ★	7	MONETAIRE (FR)	29
BOARD OF TRADE	8	MOON RACER (IRE)	30
BOONDOOMA (IRE)	8	**OK CORRAL (IRE) ★**	31
BRISTOL DE MAI (FR)	9	**PEACE AND CO (FR) ★**	32
CAMPING GROUND (FR)	10	**SAPHIR DU RHEU (FR) ★**	33
CHAMPERS ON ICE (IRE)	11	SEAMOUR (IRE)	34
CHOCCA WOCCA	12	SEGO SUCCESS (IRE)	36
CLEAN SHEET (IRE) ★	13	SMOOTH STEPPER	36
COPPER KAY	14	SOME BUCKLE (IRE)	37
DAWSON CITY	14	THE SAINT JAMES (FR)	38
DUNCOMPLAINING (IRE)	15	THREE MUSKETEERS (IRE)	39
FLETCHERS FLYER (IRE)	16	TOOWOOMBA (IRE)	40
FORTHEFUNOFIT (IRE)	17	UNOWHATIMEANHARRY	41
GARDE LA VICTOIRE (FR) ★	18	VALUE AT RISK	42
GREAT TRY (IRE)	19	VIRGILIO (FR)	42
IRISH CAVALIER (IRE) ★	20	VOLNAY DE THAIX (FR)	43
JOLLY'S CRACKED IT (FR)	21	**WAIT FOR ME (FR) ★**	44
KAKI DE LA PREE (FR)	22	WELSH SHADOW (IRE)	45
KINGSCOURT NATIVE (IRE)	23	WHICH ONE IS WHICH	46
KNOCK HOUSE (IRE)	24	WILLIAM HENRY (IRE)	46
LA VATICANE (FR)	25	WINNER MASSAGOT (FR)	47
LE MERCUREY (FR)	26	ZEROESHADESOFGREY (IRE)	48

The form summary for each horse is shown after its age, colour, sex and pedigree. The summary shows the distance, the state of the going and where the horse finished in each of its races since the start of the 2014/15 season. Performances are in chronological sequence with the date of its last race shown at the end.

The distance of each race is given in furlongs. Steeplechase form figures are prefixed by the letter 'c', hurdle form figures by the letter 'h' and NH Flat race or bumper form figures by the letter 'b'.

The going is symbolised as follows: f–firm, m–good to firm; g–good, d–good to soft; s–soft; v–heavy.

Placings are indicated, up to the sixth place, by use of superior figures, an asterisk being used to denote a win and superior letters are used to convey what happened to a horse during the race: F–fell, pu–pulled up, ur–unseated rider, bd–brought down, su–slipped up, ro–ran out.

The Timeform Rating of a horse is simply the merit of the horse expressed in pounds and is arrived at by careful examination of its running against other horses. The ratings range from 175+ for the champions down to a figure of around 55 for selling platers. Symbols attached to the ratings: 'p'–likely to improve; 'P'–capable of much better form; '+'–the horse may be better than we have rated it.

A Good Skin (Ire)   c139p
6 b.g. Presenting – Trixskin (Ire) (Buckskin (Fr))
2014/15 b16s^2 h16g^4 h21d^4 h21g c24v^2 c22.5d^2 c24s* c25.5g* Apr 16

If Victoria Pendleton wants an example of how to go from a standing start to a Cheltenham winner over fences in the space of a single National Hunt season, she needn't look much further than A Good Skin. Besides three runs in Irish points (won final one), he had no experience before running in a Worcester bumper last October. He finished second that day and fourth in a couple of hurdle races over the five weeks or so that followed, all three runs being very much a means to an end. A Good Skin had six weeks off before making his handicap debut on the King George card at Kempton and, after he finished well held there, it was decided to cut to the chase and send him over fences. He ran into Catching On at Huntingdon on his first try and the talented Bandit Country on his second, but eventually got off the mark under Rules in a handicap at Ludlow that was better than the lean field would imply.

The novice handicap A Good Skin won at Cheltenham's April meeting two weeks later looked as strong beforehand as you'd expect, with four of the ten having won their previous starts. It didn't quite turn out as predicted, with tearaway leader Trickaway ensuring that he and several others failed to see the race out. A Good Skin and Candide (who the time before had beaten Ballybough Pat, who won his next two starts) certainly did though, with the former well on top by the line; Candide was more than thirty lengths clear of Trickaway in third. It's that stamina, still largely untapped, that excites us most about A Good Skin. He has plenty of room for improvement overall, given he's only six and starting just his second season under Rules, and he'll be even harder to stop once he's granted a really good test at three miles-plus. He acts on soft ground. **Tom George**

Conclusion: *Went from Rules debutant to a very useful chaser in 2014/15; unexposed over staying trips and can land a higher-end handicap over 3m+*

Amidon (Fr)   h117

5 b.g. Dom Alco (Fr) – Immage (Fr) (Bad Conduct (USA))
2014/15 b17d b16v³ h20s² h21v² h20v⁶ h20d⁶ h24.5d² h24g³ Apr 15

Le Reve won at 10/1 as a member of our *Fifty* in 2013/14 and progressed further into a smart handicap chaser last season for trainer Lucy Wadham and owner Pat Betts. The same connections are represented by Amidon who made steady progress in bumpers and over hurdles during his debut season in 2014/15 and has the makings of a better chaser. The good-topped Amidon has a good pedigree to call upon—he cost his owner €85,000 as a three-year-old and is a half-brother to the useful hurdler/chaser Son Amix out of a half-sister to the notable staying chasers L'Ami and Kelami—and he's tipped to reach a useful level in the new term.

Amidon showed fairly useful form on the last two of his six outings over hurdles, finishing two and a quarter lengths second of six to Herbert Park in a novice at Kempton and two and a quarter lengths third of nineteen to Roll On Ruby in a novice handicap at Cheltenham. Some substance was given to the form of the latter race—in which Amidon made his effort two out but couldn't quicken as well as the first two—when the runner-up Robbie Rabbit won on his next outing. As for Lucy Wadham's record with chasers, well, if you'd backed all of her runners over fences since the start of 2012 you'd have made a massive profit of £700 to a £10 level stake. Amidon stays three miles and acts on heavy going. He often wore cheekpieces in his first season, though went without any headgear at Kempton and Cheltenham. **Lucy Wadham**

Conclusion: *Fairly useful hurdler who has the makings of a better chaser (from the family of the brothers L'Ami and Kelami); stays 3m and acts on heavy going*

Keep track of the 50 with My Timeform
Make notes online and receive alerts free

at timeform.com & on the App

Aux Ptits Soins lands the Coral Cup at Cheltenham on his British debut

Aux Ptits Soins (Fr) ★   h149p
5 gr.g. Saint des Saints (Fr) – Reflexion Faite (Fr) (Turgeon (USA))
2014/15 b13.9d³ h17.4g* h21g* Mar 11

Those that attended the inaugural Timeform Cheltenham Festival Preview Evening last March were let into a little secret by Timeform's Chief Correspondent Jamie Lynch. Lynch had recently had a chat with Nick Scholfield and was told how the jockey very much fancied Aux Ptits Soins for the Coral Cup having been very impressed by the gelding in a piece of work at Wincanton. Scholfield's faith was justified when ex-French Aux Ptits Soins made a striking British debut in that highly competitive Cheltenham handicap hurdle, overcoming a lack of big-field experience and some novicey jumping, and he looks a very bright prospect for the new season. Foot and sinus problems mean Aux Ptits Soins is unlikely to be ready until the end of November, when he reportedly could return over hurdles, with the Ascot Hurdle (which the Nicholls-trained Silviniaco Conti won in 2010) having been mentioned by his trainer, though there is also a chance he could go straight over fences (tall, useful-looking sort who's sure to make a chaser). Either way, he should prove worth the wait.

In hindsight, it makes sense that a BHA mark of 139 proved lenient for Aux Ptits Soins in the Coral Cup. When he made a winning debut at Auteuil in March 2014 he had Arbre de Vie (now Timeform-rated 152) back in third, and when he followed up on his next hurdles start at the same track six months later (third in a bumper in between) he had next-time-out winners in second and fourth. Aux Ptits Soins was purchased by John Hales after that second win and sent to Paul Nicholls. Although Aux Ptits Soins didn't look short of speed over twenty-one furlongs at Cheltenham, travelling powerfully for the most part, his pedigree suggests he'll stay further still in due course; he's by the sire of such as Djakadam and Quito de La Roque out of a half-sister to the Irish Hennessy winner Quel

Esprit (who's also by Saint des Saints). As a five-year-old, Aux Ptits Soins has plenty of time on his side (his owner reportedly views him as a future Gold Cup prospect), and there should be good races to be won with him in the new season. **Paul Nicholls**

Conclusion: *Top prospect who showed smart form in three unbeaten starts over hurdles, including a success in the 21f Coral Cup on his British debut; has more to offer over timber, and also very much the type to make a chaser*

Bitofapuzzle ★ h149

7 b.m. Tamure (Ire) – Gaelic Gold (Ire) (Good Thyne (USA))
2014/15 b16.5s* h22d* h20s² h24s* h20g³ h20v* Apr 5

As part of the BHA's ongoing attempts to improve the jumps programme for mares there will be two new mares' listed chases held at Carlisle (November 29th) and Huntingdon (February 25th) this season. The races will be run over two and a half miles and worth at least £30,000, and both could come under consideration for Bitofapuzzle who has already achieved plenty in her eight starts under Rules and has the potential to take high rank as a chaser this season.

The strong, rangy Bitofapuzzle was a maiden point winner for Richard Barber (the former boss of her current trainer Harry Fry) before she won all three of her starts in bumpers, which included two listed events, one of them on her reappearance last season in November. Bitofapuzzle went on to show smart form as she won three of her five outings in mares' hurdles, beating Carole's Spirit in the Grade 2 Warfield at Ascot in January and Petite Parisienne by four and a quarter lengths in a Grade 1 mares' novice event at Fairyhouse in April either side of finishing a very close third behind Glens Melody and Polly Peachum in the David Nicholson Mares' Hurdle at Cheltenham. Bitofapuzzle gave her very upwardly-mobile yard its first Grade 1 win in the Irish race, and the form was franked when the runner-up won the Grade 1 Champion Four-Year-Old Hurdle at Punchestown the following month. As one of the highest-rated mares in training in Britain, Bitofapuzzle is expected to prove difficult to beat in mares' chases, but she may also be good enough to compete against the males, too, with the possibility that she could develop into a genuine RSA Chase contender. Bitofapuzzle is effective from two and a half miles to three miles and goes well under testing conditions, though her run on good ground at Cheltenham proved she doesn't need the mud flying. She's a prominent racer who wears a tongue tie. **Harry Fry**

Conclusion: *Grade 1-winning mare over hurdles who has the build and background to make a cracking novice chaser; effective anywhere from 2½m to 3m*

 Download the App!

Board of Trade   b105p
4 ch.g. Black Sam Bellamy (Ire) – Realms of Gold (USA) (Gulch (USA))
2014/15 b13d* b16d* Mar 18

Battle Born was a successful member of last year's *Fifty*, though unfortunately he wasn't seen out again after making a winning start over hurdles at Uttoxeter. Hopefully we'll have better luck with his close relative Board of Trade, who, like Battle Born before him, has shown plenty of promise in bumpers. He has won both his starts, in fact, and showed a good attitude when making a winning debut at Exeter in December against fellow three-year-olds. By the time Board of Trade ran again, the Exeter runner-up Wishfull Dreaming, a brother to high-class chaser Wishfull Thinking, had gone one better in a listed event at Cheltenham. Board of Trade's sights were set a little lower, and it was March before he was seen out again when beating four rivals in a steadily-run contest at Haydock. Even so, it was hard not to be impressed by the way he drew clear off the steady gallop to win by four lengths from another well-related sort, Wade Harper, brother to the World Hurdle winner Cole Harden. Board of Trade would have been well worth his place in the Grade 2 bumper at Aintree (which Battle Born had contested the year before) but he was put away after Haydock, no doubt to resume in novice hurdles in the new season.

Besides Battle Born, their dam Realms of Gold has produced four other winning jumpers, including Gold Ingot who won over hurdles for Alan King and has since gone on to be a fairly useful chaser, winning at three miles. Board of Trade, whose two starts were on good to soft ground, will stay beyond two miles himself in due course. **Alan King**

Conclusion: *Two from two in bumpers—beat next-time-out winners both times—and just the type to win more races as a novice hurdler*

Boondooma (Ire)   c141p
8 b.g. Westerner – Kissantell (Ire) (Broken Hearted)
2014/15 h20d* h20s^5 c19s^4 c17.5v^2 c16s* Dec 20

Deciding which—if any—of the *Fifty* from the previous edition of *Horses To Follow* to carry over into the latest publication is always a bone of contention, and going too soon with the likes of Many Clouds and Postponed on the Flat in recent years has been frustrating. In a rare departure—and following much deliberation—both Boondooma and Garde La Victoire are repeat inclusions this time around. Boondooma won two of his five starts last term and remains with the potential to land a valuable handicap chase for his excellent, Grand National-winning yard.

It was no surprise Boondooma proved better over fences than he was over hurdles given he's a well-made, point-winning half-brother to high-class chaser Rocky Creek.

Having caught the eye when fourth on his chasing debut at Ascot, Boondooma looked a smart prospect in his two subsequent runs last term, finishing a close second to Melodic Rendezvous in a novice at Bangor prior to scoring by twelve lengths from Ifandbutwhynot in a similar event at Haydock (jumped well) eight days later. Unfortunately Boondooma was ruled out for the rest of the season in February after undergoing surgery on a knee injury, but his trainer didn't think the problem was serious at the time and we are sure the best is yet to come from this chasing type. Boondooma is a strong traveller but he's equally as effective over two and half miles as he is over two miles, and there will be plenty of races open to him in the new season, including the Paddy Power Gold Cup at Cheltenham in November, which was mentioned as a target by his trainer last term. Boondooma has won on good ground but has raced mostly under testing conditions (acts on heavy). He usually races close up. **Dr Richard Newland**

Conclusion: *Won the last two of his three outings over fences in 2014/15 before injury intervened and can land a big handicap over 2m-2½m this term*

Bristol de Mai (Fr)   h144p
4 gr.g. Saddler Maker (Ire) – La Bole Night (Fr) (April Night (Fr))
2014/15 b14.4g⁴ b13.4g⁶ h17.9s* h16.5v* h16.5v³ h18s² h17g³ Apr 9

Nigel Twiston-Davies hasn't won a Grade 1 novice chase since Ollie Magern landed the 2004 Feltham but the yard may well be strongly represented in such events this term if all goes to plan. The scopey Blaklion is an obvious sort for chasing having shown smart form in his novice season over hurdles last term, but the yard have an equally exciting chasing prospect in four-year-old Bristol de Mai who reached a similar standard in the juvenile ranks. The ex-French Bristol de Mai won the Grade 1 Finale Juvenile Hurdle at Chepstow on his first start for Twiston-Davies—taking his hurdling record to two from two in the process—and he showed a similar level of form when placed on his final two outings last season, which included a close third to All Yours in the Grade 1 Anniversary Hurdle at Aintree. There's better to come from Bristol de Mai over timber but he looks all over the sort who will excel once sent over fences—he's a tall gelding whose dam is a sister to the fairly useful staying chasers Mi Fasol and Show Public— and it's hoped that he's switched to the larger obstacles sooner rather than later.

Bristol de Mai had two starts in bumpers and then made his winning debut over timber in a newcomers race at Auteuil in September for Guillaume Macaire. Purchased privately after the last-named run, Bristol de Mai sported the increasingly familiar two-tone green silks of Simon Munir and Isaac Souede for the first time in the Finale in December, when he tanked along and quickened to win by six lengths from the reliable Karezak. The performance understandably made him a single-figure price for the Triumph Hurdle, though defeats in a listed race at Sandown and the

Grade 2 Premier Kelso Hurdle (creditable second to Glingerburn) meant he missed the Cheltenham race (in which his owners still had the first and second!). Bristol de Mai ended the season on a positive note at Aintree and it will be a surprise if there isn't better to come in the 2015/16 campaign. He's a strong traveller who stays two and a quarter miles and acts on heavy going. **Nigel Twiston-Davies**

Conclusion: *Bordered on smart as a juvenile hurdler (Grade 1 winner) and can do at least as well over fences; strong traveller who stays 2¼m, though pedigree gives hope he may get further*

Camping Ground (Fr)   h152 c149p

5 b.g. Goldneyev (USA) – Camomille (Ger) (Pennekamp (USA))
2014/15 c20.5v* h16.5d⁴ Mar 7

It took only a couple of starts for his new stable for French recruit Camping Ground to prove himself equally smart over both hurdles and fences, and connections must be looking forward to enjoying a fuller campaign with a five-year-old who has plenty more to offer. Sent off favourite for a handicap chase at Warwick on his British debut in February, Camping Ground overcame an absence of the best part of a year, as well as top weight, to beat his six rivals in good style with a bold round of jumping from the front. A month later, carrying top weight again but this time over the smaller obstacles, Camping Ground ran a cracker to be beaten two lengths into fourth behind Ebony Express in a big field for the Imperial Cup at Sandown, conceding more than a stone to the three who beat him. Camping Ground had previously progressed well for Joel Boisnard in France where he had completed an unusual hat-trick in his last three outings there. Those wins came in a chase for three-year-olds at Auteuil, an amateur riders event on his Flat debut and then a win over hurdles (his third in all) back at Auteuil.

Camping Ground stays two and a half miles and acts on heavy ground, with most of his races having been on ground softer than good. He has worn a tongue tie for his two starts in Britain. There could be more to come from Camping Ground over hurdles, but he makes more appeal over fences, being a lengthy, useful-looking gelding by the same sire as Balder Succes. His handicap mark means he'll have little option but to contest some valuable races, and he can raise the profile further for his Dorset yard which had a winner at Aintree on Grand National day with another French import, Astre de La Cour. **Robert Walford**

Conclusion: *Smart young jumper who can build on the promise of just two starts in Britain to date, with the potential to pick up a good handicap; stays 2½m*

The well-regarded grey Champers On Ice (carrying Bryan Drew's colours) makes a winning debut at Punchestown

 ## Champers On Ice (Ire)   b117p
5 gr.g. Robin des Champs (Fr) – Miss Nova (Ra Nova)
2014/15 NR :: 2015/16 b18s* Apr 29

While the number of horses in the ownership of Professor Caroline Tisdall and Bryan Drew is a far cry from the huge strings owned by the likes of J. P. McManus, the pair are no strangers to shelling out big sums at the sales. The £450,000 paid for Un Temps Pour Tout raised several eyebrows at the time, whilst Moon Racer cost £225,000 after he'd made a winning debut at Fairyhouse in the spring of 2014. The pair may well consider the money well spent, however, with the former developing into a high-class stayer over timber (landed the French Champion Hurdle in June), while the latter looks a fine hurdling prospect on the back of his success in last season's Champion Bumper at Cheltenham. Moon Racer has duly made it into this year's *Fifty*, and he's not the only one of his owners' big-money recruits at David Pipe's Pond House stables who we expect to make a big splash over hurdles in the new season.

We've only seen Champers On Ice—winner of an Irish point-to-point earlier in the year—once under National Hunt rules, that coming in a bumper at the Punchestown

Festival in late-April. In one of the best finishes of the entire week, he narrowly got the better of First Figaro to pay off the first instalment of his £205,000 purchase price. Having travelled powerfully throughout, Champers On Ice knuckled down really well in the closing stages to get home by a head, the pair pulling twenty-eight lengths clear of the third. That Champers On Ice was sent off 9/4 favourite that day is a measure of his lofty reputation, and the form was a given a boost when First Figaro went one better in a bumper at the Galway Festival three months later. Although he'll excel as a chaser in time, hurdling is the immediate focus for Champers On Ice, and he has the potential to take high rank in the novice division in 2015/16. He'll stay at least two and a half miles. **David Pipe**

Conclusion: *Point winner who comes with a big reputation after costing plenty at the sales; showed smart form when making a winning start in a bumper at the Punchestown Festival and looks a fine hurdling prospect*

Chocca Wocca   b106

5 b.m. Kayf Tara – Chomba Womba (Ire) (Fourstars Allstar (USA))
2014/15 b14s* b17g² Apr 11

There has been a drive in recent years to encourage owners to purchase mares for jumping in Britain by enhancing the attractiveness of the mares' jumps programme (Britain is still trying to catch up with Ireland in that respect). In July it was announced that there will be a new race run as the sixth event on the Thursday of the 2016 Cheltenham Festival, namely a Grade 2 novice hurdle for mares over seventeen furlongs which will carry a prize fund of £75,000. A mares' chase at the Festival could even follow. With these increased opportunities in mind, we've included a handful of mares among this year's *Fifty*, including Chocca Wocca who is under the care of arguably the best trainer of female jumpers in Britain, Nicky Henderson.

Chocca Wocca is the first foal out of Chomba Womba who was a prolific winner in bumpers and over hurdles, first for Mags Mullins in Ireland and then, having been bought for £160,000 by owner-breeders Richard and Lizzie Kelvin-Hughes, for Henderson for whom she won three Grade 2s, including the Elite Hurdle and the Ascot Hurdle. Having smoothly landed the odds on her bumper debut at Ludlow last December, Chocca Wocca stepped up appreciably on that form when one and three quarter lengths second of nineteen to the more experienced Hollies Pearl in a listed mares' bumper at Aintree's Grand National meeting four months later. Chocca Wocca was tackling a three-furlong longer trip (seventeen furlongs) at Aintree and ran a cracker, making headway on the home turn and keeping on after challenging over two furlongs out. Boasting a fine pedigree and in excellent hands, Chocca Wocca looks sure to make her mark over hurdles this season. **Nicky Henderson**

Conclusion: *Showed useful form in a pair of bumpers and can at least match that level over hurdles; could even be one for the new mares' novice hurdle at the Cheltenham Festival*

Clean Sheet (Ire) ★   h139P

6 b.g. Oscar (Ire) – High Park Lady (Ire) (Phardante (Fr))
2014/15 h16.5s² h16.5s* h20.5d* Feb 13

The chasers at Seven Barrows may have disappointed for the second successive campaign—the yard managed a paltry fifteen victories over fences during the whole of 2014/15—but the exploits of the stable's hurdlers ensured Nicky Henderson still finished a clear second in the trainers' championship with one hundred and twenty-nine winners, which were achieved at an impressive strike rate of 26%. Peace And Co leading home a one, two, three for the yard in the Triumph was obviously the highlight, but there were also Grade 1 wins for the novice L'Ami Serge and the seasoned stayer Whisper, as well as notable successes for novices such as Vyta du Roc and Theinval. Another novice, Clean Sheet, did his bit for the yard's strike rate lower down the chain, landing both his starts following a promising debut, and he looks a very bright prospect indeed for the new season.

A four-length winner over Kilcooley (now a very smart hurdler for Charlie Longsdon) on his sole start in points for Enda Bolger in March 2013, Clean Sheet was subsequently snapped up by J. P. McManus and made his debut over timber in a novice at Sandown twenty-one months later. Well backed, Clean Sheet shaped well in beating all bar his less-fancied stable companion Caracci Apache, whose greater experience was arguably the difference in a close finish. The form proved strong with both the winner and third (Aso) going on to score at Grade 2 level. Clean Sheet, on the other hand, was kept to calmer waters. Although only getting up by a short head in a minor event at Newbury three weeks after Sandown, he did well to overcome a couple of sloppy jumps in the straight in a race that the Henderson yard has farmed in recent years, saddling a remarkable eight of the last nine winners. Clean Sheet looked a lot more polished all round when running out an easy winner of a novice at Fakenham on his final outing in February, ridden more prominently upped to two and a half miles and scoring easily after pressing on three out. A full brother to the useful Nelson's Bridge, who won in bumpers and over timber during his sole season on the track for Seven Barrows, Clean Sheet should be better suited by two and a half miles than shorter, and he may well stay further still when required. A tall sort, he starts the new season with a Timeform large 'P' attached to his rating, suggesting he'll prove capable of much better form, and he appeals as the type to thrive in good-quality handicaps; he's well worth following from a lenient-looking initial mark of 135. **Nicky Henderson**

Conclusion: *Created a very good impression in three outings in debut campaign which spanned little more than two months; type to rate much higher in the new season and already on the radar for high-end handicaps over 2½m+*

Copper Kay   b97+

5 b.m. Kayf Tara – Presenting Copper (Ire) (Presenting)
2014/15 b16v* b16.5d⁴ Mar 7

Philip Hobbs trained Presenting Copper to win a bumper and five races over hurdles and fences for owner Alan Peterson and the trainer is already one third of the way to repeating the feat with the mare's first foal, Copper Kay, who also carries Peterson's colours. Copper Kay made a successful debut in bumpers at Warwick in January and then improved to finish five and a half lengths fourth of sixteen to Babylone des Motte in a mares' listed bumper at Sandown two months later. Copper Kay shaped better than the bare result in the latter race, not settling fully (still green) and hampered and outpaced three furlongs out before keeping on well inside the final furlong. The form looks sound with the fifth-placed Robins Reef winning a bumper on her next start and the winner running to a similar level when fifth in a similar race at Aintree, whilst the eighth Surtee du Berlais made a successful hurdling debut on her next outing. A good-looking sort who hails from a good jumping family—Presenting Copper is a half-sister to the smart hurdler/chaser at up to twenty-one furlongs Copper Bleu (also trained by Hobbs for Peterson) and the useful hurdler/chaser at up to three miles Cloudy Copper—Copper Kay looks a useful prospect for novice hurdling this season. **Philip Hobbs**

Conclusion: *Showed plenty of promise in two bumper starts and very much bred to make a jumper; can win novice hurdles (especially against her own sex) for a yard which knows her family well*

Dawson City   h124

6 b.g. Midnight Legend – Running For Annie (Gunner B)
2014/15 h20d h21.5v⁴ h19.5s h24.5s* h25.5v* h23.5v² h25s² Mar 30

'Klondike Nugget & Ivory Shop', 'Maximilian's Gold Rush Emporium' and 'Diamond Tooth Gerties' gives you an idea as to what sort of place the Canadian town of Dawson City is. Dawson City has a population of just 1,500 people and looks like a 'Land That Time Forgot' given all the buildings appear as though they're from the nineteenth century and any new constructions must comply with visual standards to ensure conformity. The gelding Dawson City is a bit of a throwback himself, an old-fashioned chasing type who's very much bred to jump fences being by Midnight Legend out of a Gunner B mare (who's other known offspring was a three-mile chase winner). Dawson City's trainer Polly Gundry knows plenty about decent staying chasers, too, as she won the 2002 Fox Hunters' Chase at Aintree on the Paul Nicholls-trained Torduff Express and also saddled Fort View to finish fifth in the same race in 2011 within weeks of launching a new career as a National Hunt trainer.

Dawson City—who shares his name with a gelding Mick Easterby trained to win the Dipper Novices' Chase in 1993—got off the mark at the fourth time of asking over timber at Taunton in December, with the catalysts for his improvement being the switch to a handicap and the step up to three miles, and he followed up off an 8 lb higher mark over three and a quarter miles at Plumpton four weeks later. Dawson City ran well to finish runner-up in similar races on his subsequent outings, on both occasions rallying and leaving the impression a greater test of stamina will suit. As an out-and-out stayer who relishes testing conditions, a switch to fences—and particularly long-distance chases—should show Dawson City in an even better light in the new season, when he could well be a potential contender for some of the regional 'Nationals'. **Polly Gundry**

Conclusion: *Fairly useful sort over hurdles who can rank higher over fences this season; thorough stayer (acts well under testing conditions) and could land one of the regional 'Nationals'*

Duncomplaining (Ire)   b95+

6 b.g. Milan – Notcomplainingbut (Ire) (Supreme Leader)
2014/15 b16d⁴ b17g⁶ Apr 10

William Kinsey has won five races with Alpha Victor, including a twenty-runner handicap hurdle at Aintree in 2012. Alpha Victor showed he could still produce useful form last season, but he also suggested that he may have had enough of racing when he took little interest in the Eider Chase and refused at the last in the Irish Grand National on his final two starts. So, Kinsey's small Cheshire-based yard is in need of another stable star—step forward Duncomplaining who is owned by one of Alpha Victor's owners, David Wesley-Yates, whose colours were most famously carried by the popular grey Monet's Garden. Duncomplaining is still a maiden after three starts in bumpers but he's shown enough—including in a Grade 2—to think he will prove profitable to follow once switched to hurdles in the new season.

Duncomplaining ran to a fairly useful level when runner-up on his bumper debut at Sedgefield in January 2014 and matched that form when fourth in a similar race at Newcastle on his next outing over thirteen months later. It was probably no coincidence that Duncomplaining then ran in the big bumper at the Grand National meeting given Monet's Garden was a regular fixture at Aintree over the years (won the Melling Chase and three renewals of the Old Roan Chase). Duncomplaining ran well for a 100/1 shot as he finished sixth of nineteen to Barters Hill, proving strong at the finish.

Duncomplaining is out of a mare who won a listed hurdle over two and a half miles (before scoring over fences) and is a half-sister to the useful chaser at up to three miles Force Seven; he'll stay at least two and a half miles over jumps himself. **William Kinsey**

Conclusion: *Showed promise in bumpers (including when sixth to Barters Hill in the Grade 2 at Aintree) and bred to make a jumper; will stay 2½m+*

Dan Barber, Jumps Editor (Duncomplaining):
"Duncomplaining went winless in bumpers, but that maiden status shouldn't put anyone off following the imposing six-year-old as he embarks on a novice hurdling campaign. Nothing finished Aintree's Champion Bumper with more purpose than Duncomplaining, his never-nearer sixth to Barters Hill that day very much catching the eye, and he should have little trouble winning races over longer distances in the North—his dam was a very useful hurdler and it would be no shock if Duncomplaining reached a similar rung on the ladder."

Fletchers Flyer (Ire) h138
7 b.g. Winged Love (Ire) – Crystal Chord (Ire) (Accordion)
2014/15 b18g* h20s³ h22s* h22v* h24s² :: 2015/16 h24s^pu Apr 29

"He is a real stayer in the making and whatever he does over hurdles this year will be a bonus as he will be jumping fences in twelve months' time." Harry Fry made it explicit that Fletchers Flyer's hurdling campaign in 2014/15 was about marking time, and as an Irish point-winning full brother to three-mile-winning chaser Three Chords with plenty of size about him, the gelding looks nailed-on to make a better chaser. Fletchers Flyer can win a good race or two on his way to the major Festivals this term, when the RSA Chase or National Hunt Chase (he'll probably stay beyond three miles) at Cheltenham could come under consideration for him.

Fletchers Flyer won his point in March 2013 and built on his bumper debut at Uttoxeter (second, had reportedly had a wind operation beforehand) the following March when winning a similar event at the 2014 Punchestown Festival under an aggressive ride. Having perhaps just needed the run when third on his hurdling debut last October in what proved a warm maiden at Ffos Las (collared by Shantou Bob and Padge), Fletchers Flyer won his next two starts in novices at Ascot in November and Wincanton in January. Fletchers Flyer went with zest and led at the fifth in the last-named race and his jockey Nick Scholfield said: "Most of the other lads came in and said 'what a gallop' but it felt pretty easy on him." Fletchers Flyer improved further on his following outing when a half-length second of seven to Definitly Red in the Grade 2 Prestige Novices' Hurdle at Haydock in February, rallying after not fluent at the last. Although Fletchers

Flyer disappointed on his subsequent outing, when pulled up in the Grade 1 novice won by Killultagh Vic at Punchestown, the promise of his previous starts shouldn't be forgotten. Fletchers Flyer races prominently and wears a tongue tie. He's clearly very effective under testing conditions, though his bumper win was achieved on good ground. **Harry Fry**

Conclusion: *Won a bumper and two hurdle races (also Grade 2 placed) but his true calling lies over fences (point winner) and will do well as a novice chaser; goes well in the mud, and will probably stay beyond 3m*

Forthefunofit (Ire) h134p

6 b.g. Flemensfirth (USA) – Sommer Sonnet (Ire) (Taipan (Ire))
2014/15 h21d³ h20.5v* h20.5d Mar 13

The J. P. McManus-owned, Jonjo O'Neill-trained Get Me Out of Here finished runner-up on no fewer than four occasions at the Cheltenham Festival, including very narrow defeats in the 2010 Supreme Novices' (beaten a head by Menorah), the 2011 County Hurdle (went down by a nose to Final Approach) and the 2014 Coral Cup (short-headed by Whisper). The same connections' six-year-old Forthefunofit may have disappointed on his first outing at the Festival when finishing down the field in the Martin Pipe last season, but he'd progressed well in winning two of his previous three outings over timber and appeals as the type who will make a much greater impact in big handicaps in 2015/16—he may even return to Cheltenham as a key Coral Cup contender.

Runner-up on both his starts in bumpers prior to a smooth success in a Catterick novice on his hurdling debut in December 2013, Forthefunofit needed the run when third to Ulzana's Raid (who followed up off a 7 lb higher mark) in a handicap over the Coral Cup course and distance on his reappearance last October. After another four months off, he got back to winning ways in a similar race at Huntingdon on his next outing, showing useful form as he won cosily by a length and a half from Party Rock. Forthefunofit didn't shape as badly as his finishing position of fifteenth suggests in the Martin Pipe, going well for a long way and still on the bridle approaching two out, and that first experience of the hurly-burly of a big-field handicap is unlikely to have been lost on him. Forthefunofit could switch to fences in the coming months—he's by the sire of such as Imperial Commander and Flemenstar—but there's unfinished business with him over timber first and he's one to follow in handicaps at around two and a half miles (stays twenty-one furlongs). He acts on heavy ground. **Jonjo O'Neill**

Conclusion: *Still unexposed after just four starts over hurdles (won twice) and can land a good-quality handicap at around 2½m, while he also has chasing potential; strong traveller who acts on heavy going*

Garde La Victoire (Fr) ★ h151

6 b.g. Kapgarde (Fr) – Next Victory (Fr) (Akarad (Fr))
2014/15 h17g³ h16.5s* h16d⁵ h19.5s⁴ h16.5v* Jan 31

As alluded to in the earlier entry on Boondooma, Garde La Victoire is our second repeat entry in this year's *Fifty*. While we're always keen to avoid repetition, we hope you agree that we have good reason in the case of Garde La Victoire who featured among our selections for 2014/15 chiefly as a top novice chase prospect only to remain over hurdles. Following a successful second campaign over timber, his yard has confirmed that Garde La Victoire will now switch to fences in the new season.

Garde La Victoire proved profitable to follow last season as he won the Grade 3 Greatwood Handicap (10/1) at Cheltenham and a listed event (11/4) at Sandown from five starts. He also ran creditably in two runs at Ascot between those wins, finishing fifth of eighteen to Bayan in the valuable Ladbroke Handicap, when conceding at least 7 lb to the rest of the field, and fourth to Baradari in a Grade 2 handicap when attempting to give 20 lb to the winner. It proved well worth connections keeping Garde La Victoire over timber for another season, the gelding reaching a smart level and bringing home over £80,000 in prize money. As a 150+ rated hurdler with the physique of one who will do better still over fences, he looks in prime position to take high rank among the novice chasers this term. We think Garde La Victoire can prove another top chaser for connections which have been responsible for such as Captain

Garde La Victoire leads over the last in the Greatwood Hurdle

Chris (Arkle winner), Menorah (also a Grade 1 winner as a novice chaser) and Wishfull Thinking (JLT runner-up) in recent years. Garde La Victoire is effective from two miles to two and a half miles. He acts on ground ranging from good to heavy. **Philip Hobbs**

Conclusion: *Smart hurdler whose strapping physique suggests he can prove at least as good over fences; could take high rank in the novice 2m-2½m division for connections that know all about top chasers*

Adam Brookes, Deputy Publications Editor
(Garde La Victoire): *"He's thoroughly genuine, has shown smart hurdles form from two miles to two and a half miles, acts on a variety of ground, is under the care of a top trainer and looks all over the sort to make a chaser; what's not to like about Garde La Victoire? He can rise to the top bracket among the novice chasers this term."*

Great Try (Ire)   h129

6 b.g. Scorpion (Ire) – Cherry Pie (Fr) (Dolpour)
2014/15 b17g⁴ h17d² h16.5s³ h17s* h20d² Mar 7

"England have got plenty of options now as Bracken opens up and finds Tindall. Now does Tindall have the pace to go? It's a foot race for the line, Tindall can't make it. Hickey makes the tackle but Hill is there, Worsley, wonderful hands, Cohen, wonderful try—it's a classic, it's an absolute classic!" Now, that was a great try—a nine-pass team effort by England against Ireland at Twickenham in 2002—and there will surely be more at the 2015 Rugby World Cup which is due to climax just as the core jumps season commences. With rugby likely to be in the headlines more than usual, it would perhaps be a very apt time for the equine Great Try, a six-year-old gelding in the care of champion trainer Paul Nicholls, to make a bigger name for himself.

Great Try was well regarded as a bumper horse—he was under consideration for the 2014 Champion Bumper after making a winning debut—and he delivered on his early promise in races over timber. Great Try won at the third time of asking in a Bangor novice in February and progressed again when two lengths second of seventeen to his stablemate As de Mee in a typically well-contested final of the long-standing EBF 'National Hunt' Novices' Hurdle series at Sandown. Paul Nicholls had actually said prior to the latter race that he though Great Try was "probably the better handicapped of my two". Great Try typically travelled strongly held up at Sandown but just lacked the pace of the winner from the last flight, keeping on in the manner of a horse who will stay even further than two and a half miles. This son of Scorpion may have more to offer as a hurdler, but as a tall, useful-looking sort out of a half-sister to the high-class chaser The Nightingale (also trained by Paul Nicholls), his future lies over fences and it's anticipated that he'll be switched to chasing sooner rather than later. **Paul Nicholls**

Conclusion: *Did well over hurdles and very much the type to make a chaser; strong traveller who'll stay beyond 2½m and could develop into a smart handicapper for his excellent yard*

Irish Cavalier (Ire) ★   c151+

6 gr.g. Aussie Rules (USA) – Tracker (Bustino)
2014/15 c19s³ c19s² c21s³ c20.5g* c25g^F :: 2015/16 c25d⁴ c21d² May 1

There aren't many horses that run twice at the same spring Festival—Battle Group scoring twice at the Grand National meeting at Aintree in 2013 is a notable recent example—and even fewer who run better on their latter start. Irish Cavalier did just that when he finished second to Blood Cotil in a big-field handicap chase for novices on the penultimate day of the latest Punchestown Festival, just three days after finishing four and a quarter lengths fourth of five to Valseur Lido in the Grade 1 Champion Novices' Chase on the first day of the meeting. Irish Cavalier had also appeared at the other two big spring Festivals in a full first campaign over fences, landing the listed novices' handicap over two and a half miles at Cheltenham prior to falling at the fifth in the Grade 1 Mildmay Novices' Chase at Aintree. Irish Cavalier appeals as the type to do better still as a chaser in 2015/16 and looks a live contender for all the big two-and-a-half-mile handicap chases, starting off with the Paddy Power Gold Cup at Cheltenham's Open meeting in November.

Irish Cavalier went a long way in a relatively short amount of time as a novice last term, quickly surpassing his useful hurdles form, and he broke his duck in the aforementioned Cheltenham race—where he beat Thomas Crapper by two and a half lengths—on just his fourth start over fences. Irish Cavalier seemed to benefit from the application of cheekpieces that day and he continued in them on his subsequent three outings, including when sticking to his task behind Blood Cotil. Irish Cavalier's jumping looks a real asset and will continue to stand him in good stead, especially when taking on seasoned rivals in the big handicaps. The good-topped Irish Cavalier wasn't beaten far over twenty-five furlongs behind Valseur Lido at Punchestown—running creditably on form—though he's at least as effective around two and a half miles. He acts on heavy going, though clearly doesn't need such conditions to show his form (his Cheltenham win came on good ground). **Rebecca Curtis**

Conclusion: *Went a long way in a short space of time as a novice chaser and looks tailor-made for valuable 2½m handicaps such as the Paddy Power Gold Cup; likeable type whose jumping is a real asset*

Jolly's Cracked It (Fr)   h137

6 b.g. Astarabad (USA) – Jolly Harbour (Rudimentary (USA))
2014/15 h16g* h16s* h16.5v² h16.5d⁵ h20.5d h16.5g⁶ Apr 10

On the face of it Jolly's Cracked It didn't quite deliver on his early promise last season having landed his first two starts over timber and then finished a good second to L'Ami Serge in the Grade 1 Tolworth Novices' Hurdle at Sandown. There were mitigating circumstances for some of his later efforts, however, and we think he can get right back on track after a summer break. Jolly's Cracked It could still make an impact in good-quality handicap hurdles this time around—his mark has been dropped by 2 lb to 138—but we'd prefer to see him sent over fences as he looks the sort to make a chaser. In excellent hands, he could well develop into a live contender for the Grand Annual at the Cheltenham Festival, which has gone to a novice seven times this century.

Jolly's Cracked It won on his third start in bumpers (his sole outing in the 2013/14 season) and resumed in the latest season with a brace of wins over hurdles, both in novices at Ascot in November. He progressed to a useful level when second of the three finishers in the Tolworth—which remains his best piece of form—before the wheels came off somewhat. Jolly's Cracked It couldn't enhance the good record of

Jolly's Cracked It looks a fine chasing prospect

novices in the Betfair Hurdle on his handicap debut, but he found himself too far back and was hardly disgraced in finishing fifth of the twenty-three runners, whilst at Cheltenham he simply didn't get home upped to two and a half miles in the Martin Pipe Handicap for conditional jockeys. There were few excuses when a well-held sixth to Cyrus Darius in the Top Novices' Hurdle at Aintree on his final outing admittedly, though he clearly wasn't himself that day.

The well-made Jolly's Cracked It is an enthusiastic type and may prove best at around two miles, at least until he's learned to relax fully (is bred to stay further). He acts on heavy going, though doesn't need testing ground to show his best (his trainer stated before the Betfair that the better ground there would suit him). **Harry Fry**

Conclusion: *Well held at Cheltenham and Aintree but remains with potential and can make a deeper mark as a novice chaser this term; enthusiastic type and may prove best at around 2m for the time being*

Kaki de La Pree (Fr)   c138p
8 b.g. Kapgarde (Fr) – Kica (Fr) (Noir Et Or)
2014/15 c24v³ c24v² c25v² Jan 31

If Tom Symonds hasn't yet delivered on the expectations put upon him when he left Nicky Henderson, it's because the bar was set so high. Symonds has started effectively from scratch, with the exception of owners Sir Peter and Lady Gibbings, former owners with Henderson who gave him some early exposure with Duc de Regniere. To reach the next level, Symonds needs a breakthrough horse and among those currently in his yard we reckon it's the Gibbings-owned Kaki de La Pree that is likeliest to take on the role.

Like Duc de Regniere, Kaki de La Pree came from Nicky Henderson. His move wasn't so much a transfer as a fire sale: bought by Michael Buckley for £115,000 after winning an Irish point, he made just one start for Henderson before being sold on to Symonds for just £13,000 ahead of the 2013/14 season. It didn't even take much patience for Symonds to turn him into a useful prospect; he finished a length second to King's Palace on his hurdling debut and would win his next two starts, including a Pertemps Qualifier. It's as a chaser that Kaki de La Pree was always likely to excel and, despite not winning in three starts last season, he soon showed himself superior over fences. He finished second to Gevrey Chambertin in a handicap at Newbury then lost out to Ned Stark by only a neck in the Towton at Wetherby, despite losing ground at the start.

As a result of light campaigning last season, Kaki de La Pree faces this winter with both his BHA mark (135) and novice status preserved. He could compete in graded novices and even be aimed at the National Hunt Chase, but given he's been campaigned mainly in the mud so far, staying handicaps seem a more likely option. As one who looks to have as much stamina as class, he could be well suited to the likes of the Welsh National and Eider. **Tom Symonds**

Conclusion: *Lightly-raced staying chaser who is likely to pick up a few novices/handicaps through the winter; possible type for the big marathon handicap chases*

Phil Turner, Jumps Handicapper (Kaki de la Pree):
"Kaki de La Pree is still waiting for his first win over fences, but he's definitely one I'll be looking out for in 2015/16. He had the misfortune to bump into Gevrey Chambertin on a rare "going day" when runner-up in a hot novice handicap at Newbury last winter, whilst he was then done absolutely no favours by the starter when a narrow second to Ned Stark in the Towton at Wetherby. With a lenient-looking BHA mark of 135, plus the option of dipping back into novice chases, it shouldn't be long before Kaki de La Pree breaks that duck."

 ## Kingscourt Native (Ire) h132p
7 b.g. King's Theatre (Ire) – Freydis (Ire) (Supreme Leader)
2014/15 b17d² h21.5d³ h21v^F h24.5s* h21v³ Feb 7

The Colin Tizzard yard had a good bunch of staying novice hurdlers last season, including Native Ruler, Robinsfirth and the best of them, Thistlecrack, who landed the three-mile Grade 1 Sefton Novices' Hurdle at Aintree and looked unlucky not to follow up in the equivalent race at Punchestown won by Killultagh Vic. This makes the following quote from the trainer—given in January—all the more interesting: "We are very excited about Kingscourt Native. He's a really nice prospect who we are going to try and turn into a Cheltenham horse for the Albert Bartlett Novices' Hurdle." Kingscourt Native didn't make the Festival, the plug being pulled after his disappointing third at Warwick in February—the first blip of his career—but he'd looked a very useful prospect when winning a Kempton novice the time before and he can get back on the up in the new season, especially if switched to chasing.

A narrow second at Exeter on his sole start in bumpers, Kingscourt Native shaped encouragingly on his hurdling debut when third behind Thomas Brown and Vago Collonges at the same track on his return last November. That form worked out well and Kingscourt Native would have opened his account in a maiden at Warwick five weeks later but for falling at the last, clear of such as Kylemore Lough and Carningli (who both went on to show useful form) at the time. Kingscourt Native gained compensation at Kempton in mid-January when he scored by nine lengths from Relentless Dreamer, unsurprisingly having no problem with the step up to an extended three miles.

A winning pointer, it's highly encouraging that Kingscourt Native quickly reached a useful level over timber as he looks the sort to make at least as good a chaser. A tall, useful-looking gelding, he's by one of the best jumps sires in recent history, King's Theatre, out of a mare by Supreme Leader; the same direct cross has produced the likes of useful chasers Carrigmartin, Cogry and Kings Lad (trained by Colin Tizzard). He's one to follow in novice chases. **Colin Tizzard**

Conclusion: *Useful novice hurdler whose physique and breeding suggests he'll prove at least as good over fences (well-regarded sort, too); stays three miles and acts on soft ground*

Knock House (Ire) c138+
6 ch.g. Old Vic – Lady's Gesture (Ire) (Anshan)
2014/15 c21.5g* c24.5s⁴ c20.5g² c20.5g⁵ c24d* Apr 6

What can £10,000 get you these days? Well, depending on the time of year it will allow you to spend a week at Knock House, the principal house on the Benmore Estate which is a famous deer forest situated in the heart of the Isle of Mull. You will need to self-cater but the price does include house staff and all activities. A similar amount would have also got you the yearling who later became Knock House when he passed through the ring in 2010 (he sold for €12,500). Knock House has already proven himself value for money with four wins, and he looks the sort to land a nice prize in the new season.

Mick Channon and owners Tim and Camilla Radford showed the regard in which they hold Knock House by running him (as a 50/1-shot) in the 2014 Neptune Novices' Hurdle, and in 2014/15 the gelding matched his useful hurdles form when winning two of his five starts over fences. Knock House made a successful chasing debut in a novice at Fakenham last October, hammering next-time-out winner Top Totti by eighteen lengths in a race which also featured Broadway Buffalo (fourth) who went on to show smart form. Knock House bounced back from a poor run at Cheltenham (fourth of five to Kings Palace) when second of nine to Stellar Notion on his handicap debut over fences in a novice event at Kempton, and he again ran creditably after eleven weeks off when fifth of twenty to Irish Cavalier in the listed handicap for novices at the Cheltenham Festival. Knock House signed off for the season with a routine success at odds on in a three-runner novice at Huntingdon.

Knock House has the potential to do better still over fences in 2015/16, when he resumes off a BHA chase mark of 138. He can land a good-quality handicap at between two and a half miles and three miles (seems to stay that far and is by Old Vic out of mare who stayed three miles over hurdles). A prominent racer, Knock House acts on heavy going, though is equally as effective on good ground. **Mick Channon**

Conclusion: *Matched his useful hurdles form in novice campaign over fences and can do even better this time around; sound jumper and one to note for good-quality handicaps at 2½m-3m*

La Vaticane (Fr)   h132p c118p

6 gr.m. Turgeon (USA) – Taking Off (Fr) (Kahyasi)
2014/15 h17.9s h19.4s^{pu} h17.9s h17.9s^4 h19.4s^{pu} h19.4v* h18.9s^3 c19.4v* c18.4s* h21g^2 Mar 14

There are numerous reasons to think the ex-French trained mare La Vaticane is a horse to follow this season. Firstly, she hails from one of the best yards in the country, one that has been responsible for many successful members of our *Fifty* in recent years. Secondly, she shaped with plenty of promise on her debut for the David Pipe stable when runner-up in a big-field handicap hurdle at Kempton (a consolation race for horses that had been balloted out of handicaps at the Cheltenham Festival). Thirdly, La Vaticane is versatile sort who won both of her outings over fences at Pau last winter by a combined margin of twenty-three lengths. Finally, she's still only six and remains open to improvement in both spheres.

La Vaticane had won three of her previous four starts before she joined the Pipes—including those two wins at Pau, her only starts over fences to date—and she went close to enhancing that record when beating all bar Theinval in a strongly-contested affair at Kempton, with the pair finishing seven lengths clear of the rest; the winner gave the form a big boost when following up off a 10 lb higher mark at Aintree's Grand National meeting. La Vaticane looks the type to win handicaps and a 6 lb rise to a hurdles mark of 132 seems more than fair. Owned by London-based Russian art collector Maria Bukhtoyarova, La Vaticane stays twenty-one furlongs and acts on heavy going (though her Kempton run on good ground showed she doesn't need the mud flying). She'll have plenty of options this season over both hurdles and fences, including mares' events, and the Pipe yard can be relied on to place her to best advantage. **David Pipe**

Conclusion: *Versatile and upwardly-mobile ex-French mare who was beaten only by another ahead of its mark on her first start for the Pipe stable; will pay her way over hurdles and fences*

Le Mercurey (Fr)　　　　　　　　　　　　　　　　h138p
5 b.g. Nickname (Fr) – Feroe (Fr) (Bulington (Fr))
2014/15 h16.5s h19.5s³ h20.5d Mar 13

"He'll go chasing in the autumn as a five-year-old, which is what we bought him for. He jumps fences beautifully and he's the future for us." Le Mercurey came from France with a tall reputation—and no doubt a hefty price tag—and after an encouraging, if relatively low key, first season for Paul Nicholls over timber in 2014/15 he could take off this time around.

Le Mercurey won both his completed starts over hurdles at Auteuil in late-2013 for Augustin Adeline de Boisbrunet, and was a close fourth and travelling well when falling at the same course in between in a race in which L'Ami Serge finished third. Le Mercurey didn't cut much ice on his first run in Britain twelve months later when seventh to L'Ami Serge in the Gerry Feilden Handicap Hurdle at Newbury—Nicholls had expressed his dissatisfaction at the discrepancy in the BHA marks handed to Le Mercurey (149) and L'Ami Serge (132)—but he shaped much better on his next outing when six and a quarter lengths third of eight to Baradari in a Grade 2 limited handicap at Ascot in January. Le Mercurey had been given a bit of respite by the handicapper (dropped 5 lb) and, upped in trip, he kept on well and seemed to finish with running left. Nicholls described Le Mercurey as "blooming" ahead of his run in the Martin Pipe Handicap at the Cheltenham Festival and the gelding again looked better than the bare result there, well off the pace while still travelling smoothly between three out and two out and sticking at it in the straight without having much chance of landing a telling blow. It could be that we've seen nothing like the best of Le Mercurey on these shores so far.

The useful-looking Le Mercurey looks the type to make a chaser—he's out of a chase-winning half-sister to the useful chaser Le Chablis—and can show smart form (at the least) as a novice this term. Usually tongue tied, he stays two and a half miles.
Paul Nicholls

Conclusion: *Campaigned sparingly by Paul Nicholls last season after coming from France with a big reputation and could really bloom as a novice chaser this term; stays 2½m and has raced only on ground softer than good so far*

Lessons In Milan (Ire)　　　　　　　　　　　　h135p
7 b.g. Milan – Lessons Lass (Ire) (Doyoun)
2014/15 h22s³ h19.5v* h22s* Mar 6

There are stacks of learning courses on offer in Milan, though unsurprisingly plenty of them involve fashion and design. While it's unlikely that Nicky Henderson's red tank top would go down too well on the catwalks of the Palazzo Reale, the big, rangy gelding Lessons In Milan would not look out of place at any show that celebrates form and style. He's a real cracker and has so much going for him that he just has to make our *Fifty*, especially as his exploits over hurdles so far (two wins from three starts) have been about marking time until he's switched to fences.

Lessons In Milan was successful in March 2013 on his sole outing in points in Ireland and was bought for £57,000 the following month. He made his debut for Henderson—and his new owner Trevor Hemmings—in January, when he ran with promise to finish third to his odds-on stable companion Out Sam in a novice at Ascot. Lessons In Milan didn't need to improve to easily land the odds in a small-field maiden at Lingfield in February, and he followed up in an eleven-runner handicap (BHA mark of 126) at Sandown, beating Serienschock by six lengths with the rest of the field well strung out. Lessons In Milan wasn't always fluent in the latter race but he found plenty when asked for his effort before two out and was suited by the emphasis on stamina; he'll stay three miles and beyond (Hemmings loves his staying chasers—he's owned three of the last eleven Grand National winners!). It was also encouraging that Lessons In Milan could take three races in relatively quick succession given the time he'd had off between his point win and his Rules debut. Lessons In Milan is a half-brother to four winners, including the Henderson-trained smart hurdler/fairly useful chaser The Polomoche (winner at up to three miles) and fairly useful chaser John Diamond (winner at up to twenty-one furlongs). He has the potential to develop into a smart staying chaser. **Nicky Henderson**

Conclusion: *Two from three over hurdles but a big sort whose future very much lies over fences (Irish point winner); raced only on testing ground so far and will be suited by 3m+*

Mick Jazz (Fr) h130p

4 b.g. Blue Bresil (Fr) – Mick Maya (Fr) (Siam (USA))
2014/15 h16.9s⁶ h16.9s² h16.5s³ h16.5s² Dec 29

When Mick Jazz made his British debut for Harry Fry at Newbury's Hennessy meeting he did so in the same juvenile that Fry had used to introduce another ex-French gelding, Activial, the previous year. Activial, an 8/1 shot, showed plenty that day when finishing second to Calipto in what turned out to be a strong affair, and he went on to land the Grade 2 Adonis Hurdle on his next outing. Mick Jazz, who like Activial runs in the red, pink hoop silks of Potensis Bloodstock Limited, wasn't quite as successful on the face of things in a juvenile campaign in Britain that was restricted to just two starts, but both his efforts were brimming with promise and we'll be more than a little surprised if he doesn't make a much bigger impact in his second season.

Twice-raced in big-field hurdle races at Clairefontaine in the summer of 2014 for his previous yard, Mick Jazz was seemingly well fancied by connections ahead of his British debut, sent off 7/4 second favourite behind the odds-on Karezak, and he shaped with plenty of encouragement in finishing third to Old Guard, not seeing out his race as well as the first two having gone with exuberance from the front. Markedly different tactics were adopted for Mick Jazz's subsequent outing in a similar event back at Newbury four weeks later. He started at 6/5-on and went even shorter in-running (loomed up two out after taking a strong hold in rear) before finishing second to Top Notch, who went on to win his next two outings before finishing a close second to Peace And Co in the Triumph Hurdle. Mick Jazz was due to run in the Fred Winter at the Festival—and was fancied by plenty in Timeform House to run a big race—but he wasn't quite right following a gallop two weeks beforehand and was scratched for the season. Such faith on our part hopefully won't prove misplaced in the long term; he clearly has plenty of raw ability, and it's expected that a more polished Mick Jazz will return in the autumn. Still a maiden—and therefore with his novice status still intact—connections of Mick Jazz have plenty of options open to them starting out in 2015/16, though as an exuberant sort, it may well be that the major two-mile handicaps will offer the best chance of big-race success. Whichever route is chosen, Mick Jazz is in excellent hands to have his potential realised. **Harry Fry**

Conclusion: *Burnt a few fingers on first two British starts but ran into Top Notch on latter occasion and remains with plenty of potential; strong traveller and big-field 2m handicaps may be where he really shines*

Andrew Mealor, Publications Editor (Mick Jazz):
"Although he looked far from the finished article, there was no mistaking the promise shown by the strong-travelling Mick Jazz in his two starts in Britain last winter. With a long break under his belt, there will hopefully be more end product to go with his undoubted style this term, and he'll be well worth following in two-mile events over timber."

Minella Rocco (Ire) ★   h150P
5 b.g. Shirocco (Ger) – Petralona (USA) (Alleged (USA))
2014/15 h21d* h21s* Feb 27

When Tony McCoy was asked which horse he would be most looking forward to riding in 2015/16 if he hadn't retired, he nominated two: More of That and Minella Rocco. The first needs no introduction, and McCoy's confidence in the latter looks very well founded as Minella Rocco looked a cracking prospect in winning both his starts over timber under the champion jockey last term. Minella Rocco—who will be ridden by J. P. McManus' new retained rider Barry Geraghty this season—has the potential to go right to the top, whether he is kept to hurdles or switched to fences, and if he does go chasing then current odds of 16/1 for both the JLT Novices' and RSA at the Cheltenham Festival won't last long.

Minella Rocco wasn't cheap as he cost J. P. McManus £260,000 four days after he won an Irish maiden point on his debut in March 2014. The gelding made his first start in the old green and gold in a twenty-one furlong novice hurdle at Kempton in early-February and quickened clear of the odds-on West Wizard to score by six lengths. Minella Rocco added another length onto his winning margin when landing a similar race at Newbury three weeks later, making the fairly useful runner-up Royal Vacation look utterly pedestrian and not breaking sweat himself. McCoy said about Minella Rocco: "He was very professional. He's a big horse and cost a lot of money, and you can see why. I don't think he's mentally sharp enough for Cheltenham, but we'd know more about him after another run." As it turned out Minella Rocco wasn't seen again last term—he was well fancied for the Grade 1 Sefton Novices' Hurdle at Aintree but was a non-runner on the day because he was 'sore'. Minella Rocco is a half-brother to four winners, including the smart hurdler/fairly useful chaser at up to two and a half miles Big Moment and useful chaser Pressgang (two and a half mile winner), but he's already the best of his dam's progeny. He's worn a tongue strap for both of his outings to date. *Jonjo O'Neill*

Conclusion: *Oozed class when winning both his starts in 21f novice hurdles and could be headed right to the top, whether kept over timber or switched to fences*

Monetaire (Fr) c144+
9 b.g. Anabaa (USA) – Monitrice (Fr) (Groom Dancer (USA))
2014/15 c16s^3 c17s* c21m^2 c21.5g^{ur} :: 2015/16 h20s May 2

The Pipe yard will probably be forever synonymous with innovation in racing, but they're not afraid to stick with a formula once it's shown to work. That can be seen in how they've won two, and so nearly three, of the last four runnings of the Festival Plate. There's been a handy visual reminder of Pipe's Plate successes in the form of owner Allan Stennett's beige-and-green checks, which have been common to Salut Flo, Ballynagour and Monetaire. The last-named is the only one of the three to have come up short, finishing second to Darna in March, but a big handicap success surely isn't far away.

Like Salut Flo and Ballynagour before him, Monetaire formerly raced for Stennett in France and was immediately thrown into handicap chases. He couldn't emulate them by winning on his British debut, but he was tried higher (ran at the Paddy Power meeting) and shaped well—getting to the front after two out despite a tentative display of jumping. He made no mistake at Newbury a couple of weeks later and was then put away, presumably with the intention of saving his mark for the Festival Plate. It could easily be claimed that Monetaire shaped better than Darna, too, allowing the winner a significant start turning in and just unable to peg him back in a race that yielded a fast finishing sectional. (Monetaire had also been slowly away after a restart).

Monetaire's two subsequent runs can be effectively discarded, though that he coped so well with the demands of the Topham before an unlucky unseat illustrates how far his jumping came on through the season. We expect him to continue on an upward trajectory in Pipe's care and are anticipating a big-race win for him this winter, perhaps as soon as the Paddy Power. It's not out of the question that Monetaire will be up to contesting the Ryanair, rather than the Plate, come March. He acts on soft and good to firm ground. **David Pipe**

Conclusion: *Likely type for big handicaps around 2½m on the back of promising first campaign for the yard, and could be a graded-level performer by the end of the season*

Moon Racer (Ire)   b123p
6 b.g. Saffron Walden (Fr) – Angel's Folly (Wesaam (USA))
2014/15 b16.5d* b16.5g* Mar 11

'Opportunities are never lost; someone will take the one you miss.' That adage wasn't strictly true at Goresbridge Sales in Ireland in 2010 when a yearling colt by Saffron Walden out of Angel's Folly failed to make his reserve at just €250, but the same horse did sell as an unraced four-year-old for €5,000 to owner-trainer Michael Ronayne. Moon Racer became a first winner for Dungarvan-based Ronayne—who has sent out just a handful of runners each season since 2000/01—when he made a successful debut at 50/1 in a valuable sales bumper at Fairyhouse eight months later. The next time Moon Racer was sold—at the Cheltenham April Sales in 2014—he went for £225,000 to trainer David Pipe bidding on behalf of Professor Caroline Tisdall and property developer Bryan Drew. Moon Racer went some way to justifying his price tag when carrying Drew's orange and dark blue colours to victory in a bumper at Cheltenham in October and then Tisdall's dark green, red and beige livery to success in the Champion Bumper, giving the owners their first win at the Cheltenham Festival.

Moon Racer was backed into favouritism for the Champion Bumper and he didn't let his supporters down. Different tactics were forced on Moon Racer due to a standing start (slowly into stride) but it was no bad thing as it turned out, as he made headway up the inner from three out and led over a furlong out. Moon Racer hit the line with a length and a half to spare over the runner-up Modus (eighth the previous year),

Champion Bumper winner Moon Racer is expected to take equally high rank as a novice hurdler

with the same distance back to another member of this season's *Fifty*, Wait For Me. The manner in which Moon Racer put a seal on matters left little doubt he was the best horse in the race. The good-topped Moon Racer has the physique for jumping and is as exciting a hurdling prospect as any for this season, when he's fully expected to take high rank in the novice division; he's 8/1 favourite at the time of writing in the ante-post market for both the Supreme and Neptune. The unbeaten Moon Racer has been very strong at the end of his races and, as a brother to twenty-one furlong winner Saffron Wells, he looks sure to stay further than two miles. **David Pipe**

Conclusion: *The highest-rated bumper performer trained in Britain last season after winning the Champion Bumper, and has the potential to reach the top in novice hurdles, too; will stay further than 2m*

 ## OK Corral (Ire)   b122+

5 b.g. Mahler – Acoola (Ire) (Flemensfirth (USA))
2014/15 b16d* :: 2015/16 b16g² Apr 30

For the second time in three years Nicky Henderson saddled the runner-up in the Kildare Post I.N.H Flat race, one of several bumpers at the Punchestown Festival which complement the Grade 1 Championship event at Ireland's five-day end-of-season fixture. 6/1-shot OK Corral, one of two challengers from Seven Barrows in the eight-strong field—and seemingly less fancied than his stablemate Newsworthy who went off at 4/1—stayed on well after being patiently ridden and was beaten two and a quarter lengths by the Willie Mullins-trained favourite Yorkhill; the pair pulled some seventeen lengths clear of the third and both achieved a very high level of form (Yorkhill is included on our list of horses to follow from Ireland in the following section). Two years previously, Henderson's Captain Cutter had finished second in the same race to a Mullins-trained winner when beaten nine lengths by Turnandgo in testing conditions. Captain Cutter went on to achieve notable success as a novice hurdler the following season, when unbeaten in three starts (including the Grade 1 Challow Novices' Hurdle) before having to be put down after fracturing his pelvis in the Albert Bartlett at Cheltenham. If anything, OK Corral looks an even better hurdling prospect at this stage. A €90,000 purchase from the first crop of Coolmore's promising National Hunt stallion Mahler (who finished runner-up in Lucarno's St Leger), OK Corral has plenty of size and scope about him, and he's certainly bred to excel over jumps—his dam, a winning pointer, is a half-sister to the top-class staying chaser Tidal Bay. Successful in a maiden event at Kempton in early February on his sole start prior to Punchestown, OK Corral was rated behind only Cheltenham winner Moon Racer among bumper horses trained in Britain last season, and he can take high rank among the staying novices over timber in 2015/16. **Nicky Henderson**

Conclusion: *Went a long way in just two starts in bumpers in debut season, with second to Yorkhill at Punchestown particularly strong form; looks a cracking prospect for novice hurdles over 2½m+*

Peace And Co (Fr) ★ h161P
4 b.g. Falco (USA) – Peace Lina (Fr) (Linamix (Fr))
2014/15 h16.9d* h16.5d* h17s* h17d* Mar 13

Faugheen may be a short price to retain his Champion Hurdle crown in 2016 but he's not the only unbeaten hurdler with his sights on a successful return to Cheltenham in the spring. If he makes the expected progress, Triumph Hurdle winner Peace And Co could well prove Faugheen's main rival in March. Triumph Hurdle winners sometimes struggle against their elders in their second season over hurdles, but Peace And Co looks an above-average leader of the four-year-old generation with more than the usual margin for improvement. A good-topped gelding with physical scope, he has some growing up to do mentally, too, as he showed when idling to a neck win over stablemate Top Notch at Cheltenham after travelling strongly through the race and challenging on the bridle.

Having made a winning debut over hurdles at Clairefontaine the previous summer, Peace And Co showed himself to be up to Triumph Hurdle standard right from his British debut for Nicky Henderson in December when he made a tremendous impression in beating the useful Starchitect by the best part of twenty lengths in the Summit Juvenile Hurdle at Doncaster. On his only other start before the Triumph, Peace And Co had to show grit rather than style to win another Grade 2 contest, the Finesse Juvenile Hurdle at Cheltenham. In a race run at a crawl in testing conditions, Peace And Co ran out a determined three-length winner from the useful and consistent Karezak.

Peace And Co tends to race freely and a well-run race at around two miles is likely to bring out the best in him. Whether that's good enough to win a Champion Hurdle remains to be seen, but he looks sure to remain very hard to beat along the way, as he graduates to the top two-mile hurdles at a time when credible Champion Hurdle candidates, in Britain at least, look very thin on the ground. Peace And Co has raced only on soft or good to soft ground so far. **Nicky Henderson**

Conclusion: *Above-average Triumph Hurdle winner with the potential to go right to the top as a 2m hurdler; makes appeal at 10/1 for the Champion Hurdle*

Saphir du Rheu (Fr) ★   h161 c161p

6 gr.g. Al Namix (Fr) – Dona du Rheu (Fr) (Dom Pasquini (Fr))
2014/15 c20s^{ur} c19.5d* c24g^F h24s* h24m² c25g* Apr 10

When Paul Nicholls announced at his owners' open day in September that Silviniaco Conti would be most unlikely to have a fourth crack at the Cheltenham Gold Cup in March, it was telling what he said about Saphir du Rheu. "There's no doubt in my mind he could be our next Gold Cup horse" was Nicholls' view on the gelding who won top races over both hurdles and fences in 2014/15. Saphir du Rheu hasn't finished improving yet—he's still only six after all—and ante-post odds of 16/1 about him for the 2016 Gold Cup look very attractive at this stage; while Nicholls has said the grey is "still immature" and that he doesn't want to "overface him and ask too much too soon", his exploits last season proved he's already man enough for the big stage. The Hennessy Gold Cup at Newbury—in which he would receive 9 lb from Coneygree—in late-November is said to be Saphir du Rheu's first major target, with connections considering taking in the Future Stars Intermediate Chase at Sandown or even a race over hurdles en route.

Successful in three valuable handicap hurdles in 2013/14, Saphir du Rheu didn't enjoy the best fortune on his first three goes over fences last season when he sandwiched a win in a novice at Exeter between an unseat in the Grade 2 Berkshire at Newbury and a fall in the Grade 1 Kauto Star (Feltham) at Kempton. Saphir du Rheu's mishaps appeared nothing more than that—and he'd jumped very well for his win—but he

An impressive success in the Mildmay for Saphir du Rheu

was still back over hurdles on his next outing in January. Saphir du Rheu hit the ground running—so to speak—as he won the Cleeve Hurdle at Cheltenham before improving further to beat all bar Cole Harden in a big-field World Hurdle at the same track. Saphir du Rheu went back over fences for his final start and emphatically answered any questions about his jumping with a flawless display to land the Grade 1 Mildmay Novices' Chase at Aintree; he jumped boldly and drew clear between the last two fences to beat Carraig Mor by fifteen lengths.

Having already matched his high-class hurdles form in just four runs over fences, there's an expectancy that Saphir du Rheu can go further up the ladder as a chaser this season, when he could well become the latest top-class staying chaser off the production line at Ditcheat. He's very much one to follow. **Paul Nicholls**

Conclusion: *High-class performer over hurdles and fences who has the potential to do better still over the larger obstacles; looks a Gold Cup contender for a yard who know what it takes to win that race*

 ## Seamour (Ire)   h140p
4 b.g. Azamour (Ire) – Chifney Rush (Ire) (Grand Lodge (USA))
2014/15 h17v* h16.5v* Dec 27

Classy dual-purpose horses may not be quite as common as they once were (the legendary Sea Pigeon landed two Chester Cups, an Ebor and two Champion Hurdles), though there are still ample opportunities for the right type of horse. Overturn, a Grade 1 winning hurdler who landed a Chester Cup on the Flat, did his bit for the category earlier this decade, whilst Willie Mullins has led the way among jumps trainers in the top staying races on the Flat over the past couple of years with such as Clondaw

Warrior, Max Dynamite and Wicklow Brave—all useful or better over timber—making a big splash on the level. Four-year-old Seamour has already tasted plenty of success under both codes—his combined career record is five wins from nine outings—and following a fruitful campaign on the Flat in 2015 he's expected to more than make his presence felt in good handicap company over hurdles for the excellent Brian Ellison.

Seamour started out on the level for Jo Crowley in the summer of 2014, finishing a promising second in a maiden on the polytrack at Kempton prior to landing a similar event there. Having been purchased for 110,000 guineas by current owner Phil Martin and sent to Ellison, the son of Azamour wasted little time in making his mark in juvenile hurdles. On his hurdling debut at Market Rasen, Seamour overcame obvious signs of inexperience and looked a good deal better than the bare form when scoring by eleven lengths from Pain Au Chocolat, who won his next two outings and finished fifth in the juvenile Grade 1 at Punchestown. The opposition wasn't as strong at Wetherby later in December but Seamour once again impressed as he justified favouritism with the minimum of fuss. An injury scuppered a planned outing in the Triumph Hurdle but Seamour has bolstered his profile over the summer, winning two-mile handicaps at Haydock and Ascot and finishing sixth in both the Northumberland Plate and Doncaster Cup (holds a Cesarewitch entry at the time of writing). It's hoped that Seamour's attentions are switched back to hurdling this winter as he could prove very well handicapped (missing the Triumph may prove a blessing in disguise in that regard). **Brian Ellison**

Conclusion: *Won both starts over hurdles last winter and has improved plenty on the Flat since, so potentially very well treated back over timber; stays 2m on the level and should stay 2½m+ over timber*

Jamie Lynch, Chief Correspondent (Seamour): *"Second seasons can be like second albums—very difficult—and predicting which juveniles will translate promise into achievement can be a guessing game. Fortunately, Seamour has played the game for us, raising his game again on the Flat, gamely so. What else the summer has told us is that Seamour has plenty of stamina, something yet to be mined in him as a hurdler, and, literally and figuratively, he could go a long way this season."*

Find us on Facebook
facebook.com/timeform1948

Sego Success (Ire)   c141

7 b.g. Beneficial – The West Road (Ire) (Mister Lord (USA))
2014/15 c24s⁴ c25s* c24.5v* c32g⁵ c32.5mᵖᵘ Apr 18

"Sego Success had two starts in Irish points for Adrian Maguire, finishing fourth and then winning easily in February, and is a horse we're very pleased with. He may well go straight over hurdles." Alan King was keeping his cards relatively close to his chest when he discussed Sego Success in the 2013/14 edition of *Horses To Follow*, but that the trainer gave the gelding as his 'Dark Horse' to follow showed he was held in high regard, and the promise he showed in his first season over fences in 2014/15 suggests he could be the sort to land a valuable staying handicap chase this time around.

Sego Success was a winner over hurdles, but as a good-topped Irish maiden point winner it was no surprise he rated higher—in the region of a stone, in fact—over fences last term. Sego Success improved from his chasing debut when winning a maiden at Wetherby and a listed novice at Warwick on his next two starts. Both wins came at around three miles on testing ground and he looked a real player for the 'four-miler' at the Cheltenham Festival, though in the event he shaped like he needed an even stiffer test (the pace was steady for a long way) as he finished fifth of seventeen to the former two-mile hurdler Cause of Causes. Sego Success was disappointing on his final start when pulled up in the Scottish Grand National but his stable were struggling at the time and he's tipped to get right back on track in the coming months. The Alan King yard has excelled with this type of horse—Halcon Genelardais and West End Rocker instantly spring to mind—and Sego Success looks an ideal type for races likes the Welsh National in December and Warwick Classic Chase in January. **Alan King**

Conclusion: *Plenty of promise in his first season over fences and can win a big handicap this term; should be suited by long distances and acts on heavy going, so the Welsh National looks an obvious target*

Smooth Stepper   h123

6 b.g. Alflora (Ire) – Jazzy Refrain (Ire) (Jareer (USA))
2014/15 b17d³ h17s⁴ h16.5sᵘʳ h17s* h20.5d* h16d³ h20.5vᵖᵘ h20s⁵ h24.5g Apr 17

Don't be put off by the way Smooth Stepper finished last season with some tame efforts in the spring. Several from his yard ended the campaign the same way—the yard sent out only six winners in the months of February, March and April—and in Smooth Stepper's case it should pay to overlook those races and concentrate instead on some promising performances which came in mid-season. Having shown promise in bumpers, his first win over hurdles came in a novice at Sedgefield on Boxing Day when he was prominent throughout and stayed on well to account for some better-fancied rivals. A step up in trip looked sure to suit Smooth Stepper and he duly followed up on his handicap debut at Wetherby two weeks later over two and a half miles. The gallop was only steady, and Smooth Stepper would surely have put more than two and three-quarter lengths between himself and runner-up Mr Grey had there been more pace, but he stormed clear even so.

Although third at Newcastle next time, another steadily-run race, this time over two miles, proved a completely inadequate test which led to him getting outpaced, while at the end of quite a busy campaign Smooth Stepper wasn't in the same form for his remaining races, two of which came less than a week apart. With a summer's break behind him, Smooth Stepper should be ready to bounce back in handicap hurdles at two and a half miles or more, while he would be just as interesting if connections opt to send him chasing instead. A winner on soft ground (he showed promise on his bumper debut on heavy), it was more than a lack of stamina which beat Smooth Stepper over three miles on his final start, a distance that won't necessarily prove beyond him in future as he's a half-brother to a fairly useful hurdler/chaser at around that trip in Ireland, King of Redfield. **Sue Smith**

Conclusion: *Went off the boil in the spring but had created a good enough impression during the winter to suggest there's still more to come from him, be it in handicap hurdles or as a novice chaser; should stay 3m*

Some Buckle (Ire)   h135

6 b.g. Milan – Miss Moppit (Ire) (Torus)
2014/15 b16g h16s* h16.5g² h20.5s⁵ h16.5d⁶ h20g Apr 10

Big-spending owner Roger Brookhouse enjoyed some success with his Tom George-trained chasers last season as Stellar Notion and The Ould Lad both scored twice in handicaps—the former landed a strong event at Kempton on Boxing Day—and the same connections look to have another decent chasing prospect on their hands with Some Buckle. Having shown promise in a couple of outings in bumpers, he made an instant impression over hurdles when routing some inferior rivals in a maiden hurdle at Southwell on his reappearance in December. Although Some Buckle failed to add to his tally in four subsequent starts over timber, he acquitted himself well in the face of some stiff tasks, including when sixth in an attritional renewal of the Imperial Cup, faring best of those held up in a race dominated by prominently-ridden horses. Like many of Brookhouse's horses, Some Buckle was an expensive purchase, costing the owner £180,000 after winning on his sole outing in points. A real chasing type on looks, he ought to excel over fences—he's certainly expected to improve upon his hurdles rating of 135. Some Buckle has form over two and a half miles but may prove most effective at shorter trips. He acts on soft ground. **Tom George**

Conclusion: *Point winner who is very much a chasing type in appearance, and expected to do well over fences this term having made up into a useful novice over hurdles: stays 2½m, though may prove most effective at shorter*

The Saint James (Fr)   h140 c135p
4 b.g. Saint des Saints (Fr) – Aimela (Fr) (Sagamix (Fr))
2014/15 c17.4d² c17.4s⁴ c17.9s² h16.5v⁴ h16.5g³ h20g² :: 2015/16 h20s May 2

There was arguably no bigger eye-catcher at the Cheltenham Festival than The Saint James who flew home into third in the Fred Winter under what looked a rare misjudged ride by Paul Carberry. The Saint James, a 33/1-shot making just his second start in Britain, was still off the pace three out and yet to be asked for his effort approaching the straight before finally shaken up before the last. He was also perhaps unlucky not to make amends in a competitive open handicap at Aintree four weeks later; The Saint James was bumped at the seventh, met some trouble two out and made a mistake at the last before finishing a half-length second to Theinval. His final outing last term can be overlooked—possibly finding the race coming too soon when well held in another valuable event at Punchestown—and The Saint James can get right back on track and land a valuable handicap in the new season, with the Coral Cup or even the Pertemps Final (which his trainer has won a record four times) likely to be near the top of his connections' hit-list.

The Saint James won two of his three hurdles starts for François Nicolle in France, where he also showed promise on his three outings over fences (all at Auteuil, best effort when second in a Group 2 on the final occasion). Having been purchased by J. P. McManus for €320,000 and sent to Jonjo O'Neill, The Saint James managed only fourth of five at Sandown on his first run for his new stable, but he proved a bit keen on his first start for three months and made a few mistakes. He obviously fared much better in the Fred Winter which was won by Qualando, who'd finished third to The Saint James on similar weight terms at Auteuil eleven months earlier. A useful looker, The Saint James will probably stay over hurdles for the immediate future, though his connections do have the option of returning him to fences. He stays two and a half miles and acts on heavy going (though his narrow defeats at Cheltenham and Aintree came on good ground). Usually tongue tied, The Saint James wore a hood on his last three starts. **Jonjo O'Neill**

Conclusion: *Four-year-old who went close in two valuable handicap hurdles last term and can land a good prize this time around; stays 2½m*

Three Musketeers is a very exciting chasing prospect

Three Musketeers (Ire)   h143p

5 b.g. Flemensfirth (USA) – Friendly Craic (Ire) (Mister Lord (USA))
2014/15 h22s* h21v* h20g³ Apr 11

When celebrated French author Alexandre Dumas wrote *The Three Musketeers*, he was a practising fencer who'd already written *The Fencing Master* in collaboration with his own fencing master, Augustin Grisier—there's even an Alexandre Dumas Fencing Society in New York. Fencing should also be the game for the racehorse Three Musketeers who is rated highly by his very upwardly-mobile trainer Dan Skelton and could well develop into a live contender for the RSA Chase this season.

Following a successful hurdling debut in a novice at Wetherby, it looked potentially significant that Skelton pitched Three Musketeers straight into Grade 2 company in the Leamington Novices' Hurdle at Warwick in January, and so it proved. Three Musketeers was still on the bridle three out, led before the next and, having run green and wandered between the last two hurdles, found extra towards the finish to score by three quarters of a length from Ballagh. Skelton deliberately missed the Cheltenham Festival with Three Musketeers but decided to let him take his chance at Aintree, and the gelding took another step forward as he finished eleven and a half lengths third of twelve to Nichols Canyon in the Grade 1 Mersey Novices' Hurdle. A National Hunt-bred who was runner-up on his sole start in Irish maiden points (when trained by Charlie Swan), Three Musketeers had a contrasting background to the Flat-bred pair that beat him at Aintree (Parlour Games was second), and he was essentially found wanting for pace in a race that looked barely enough of a test of stamina for him under much quicker conditions than he'd previously encountered. It was a highly promising effort all things considered, especially given his relative lack of experience. A half-brother to the useful hurdler/chaser Royal Regatta (winner at up to two and a half miles) from the family of high-class staying chaser Strong Flow, Three Musketeers is likely to stay three miles this season. He has bags of long-term potential. **Dan Skelton**

Conclusion: *Well-regarded gelding who showed plenty of ability in three starts over timber and very much one to note for novice chases over 2½m+; possible RSA contender*

Toowoomba (Ire) c118

7 b.g. Milan – Lillies Bordello (Ire) (Danehill Dancer (Ire))
2014/15 h20s³ c20s⁵ c20.5d* c20.5v* c20.5s⁴ Feb 14

Backing all of Philip Hobbs' runners in handicap chases since the start of the 2011/12 season would have yielded a profit of around £200 to a £10 level stake. One horse we feel can add to those gains this term is Toowoomba who takes his name from 'The Garden City' in Queensland, Australia. Philip Hobbs isn't a trainer who lets the grass grow under his feet and he'll surely have a suitable campaign already mapped out for Toowoomba for the coming weeks and months.

As an Irish point winner from the family of top-class staying chaser Beef Or Salmon, there was always the likelihood that Toowoomba's runs in a bumper and over hurdles were just about laying a foundation before he switched to racing over fences. Toowoomba made the transition last October and made some novicey mistakes when he finished fifth of ten in a novice handicap at Ludlow. That experience clearly wasn't lost on him as he landed his next two outings, namely an open handicap at Leicester and a novice handicap at Wincanton seven days later. In the latter Toowoomba overcame a bad mistake at the eleventh (soon came back on the bridle) when beating King of Glory (who may be worth looking out for himself this season) by four and a half lengths, the pair pulling well clear of the other five runners. Toowoomba disappointed back in open handicap company at Wincanton on his final outing, but he clearly wasn't right that day and is well worth another chance to resume his progress in the new term. A strong-travelling sort who is usually held up, Toowoomba stays two and a half miles and acts on heavy ground. **Philip Hobbs**

Conclusion: *Ended last season on a low note but had looked a young chaser on the up previously and can get back on track this season; stays 2½m*

Unowhatimeanharry h121

7 b.g. Sir Harry Lewis (USA) – Red Nose Lady (Teenoso (USA))
2014/15 h20d³ h22.5d⁴ h23.5v² h22s³ h23.5d h22s^pu Mar 6

For much of his career—and perhaps harshly in hindsight for a boxer who retired with just five defeats in forty bouts—Frank Bruno was seen as a 'loveable loser' by the wider British public; a brave but limited fighter who would always come up short at the top level. The hugely popular Bruno failed in his first three attempts at winning the world heavyweight title, including a defeat by the then-undefeated Mike Tyson in Las Vegas in 1989. Prior to being stopped on his feet in the fifth round, Bruno had rocked Tyson in the first, causing esteemed BBC commentator Harry Carpenter to briefly abandon any veneer of impartiality and roar "get in there Frank!". Bruno's popularity had been boosted by the double act the boxer had developed with Carpenter in post-fight interviews down the years, which led to the boxer's famous catchphrase "Know what I mean, 'Arry?" Carpenter had retired by the time Bruno eventually came good in a world title fight, defeating Oliver McCall on points at Wembley in 1995 to win the WBC belt, a title he would swiftly relinquish when stopped in three rounds by Tyson in their second fight a few months later. The horse whose name recalls Bruno's catchphrase, the seven-year-old gelding Unowhatimeanharry, has also been something of gallant loser so far, winless in twelve outings since a successful debut in a bumper, but a switch to the Harry Fry yard ahead of the new season could well be the catalyst for a change in fortune.

Formerly trained by Helen Nelmes, Unowhatimeanharry has developed into a fairly useful handicapper in two seasons over timber. He gave his running more often than not in the 2014/15 campaign, making the frame on four of his six outings and also running well from well out of the handicap when seventh in the Pertemps Qualifier won by Regal Encore at Exeter in February. Unowhatimeanharry can be expected to improve for the switch to Fry, one of the best young trainers in the country, and the recent example of Shuil Royale shows what Fry can do with recruits from other stables. Formerly trained by David Arbuthnot, Shuil Royale has won three of his four starts since making his debut for Fry in February, including the valuable John Smith's Summer Cup at Uttoxeter in June. Similar success hopefully awaits Unowhatimeanharry this season, when he could prove to be well treated starting back from a mark of 123. Proven up to three miles, he's raced only on ground softer than good (acts on heavy). **Harry Fry**

Conclusion: *Solid if unremarkable handicapper over timber thus far, but has changed stables over the summer and predicted to have a much more fruitful time of things this season; stays 3m*

 Follow us on Twitter @Timeform

Value At Risk   h146

6 b.g. Kayf Tara – Miss Orchestra (Ire) (Orchestra)
2014/15 b16g³ h19v* h20.5s² h24d⁵ Mar 13

Value At Risk showed smart form in bumpers when trained by Philip Fenton in Ireland, notably finishing third to Shaneshill in the Grade 1 event at the 2014 Punchestown Festival, and he achieved a similar level over hurdles for Dan Skelton last term, winning effortlessly on his seasonal return before acquitting himself with credit at a higher level on his two subsequent starts. It was perhaps slightly surprising that the stoutly-bred Value At Risk—by Kayf Tara out of 1998 Midlands Grand National winner Miss Orchestra—seemingly failed to get home on his first attempt at three miles in the Albert Bartlett Novices' Hurdle at the Cheltenham Festival, weakening into fifth having travelled smoothly, but there were mitigating circumstances. A strong gallop on rain-softened ground turned the Albert Bartlett into an unusually-gruelling affair—to the extent that eight of the nineteen runners were pulled up—and it's worth remembering that Value At Risk was making just his third outing over hurdles and only the eighth of his career. He'd certainly not looked short of stamina on his previous start when rallying to finish a close second to Ordo Ab Chao in the Classic Novices' Hurdle over an extended two and a half miles on soft ground at Cheltenham in January.

Given another summer to strengthen, Value At Risk ought to prove a different proposition the next time he tackles three miles, whilst the switch to chasing should enable him to up his game to another level, with his physique, pedigree and running style all indicating that he has what it takes to reach the top as a chaser. Having inherited Value At Risk part-way through last season, Skelton is confident that he can get more out of the lightly-raced six-year-old, and he's expected to feature prominently in some of the best novice chases this season. **Dan Skelton**

Conclusion: *Failed to get home in a gruelling renewal of the Albert Bartlett but had impressed on his previous two starts over timber, and expected to do better again over fences this term for excellent yard; bred to be suited by at least 3m*

Virgilio (Fr)   h133p c104p

6 b.g. Denham Red (Fr) – Liesse de Marbeuf (Fr) (Cyborg (Fr))
2014/15 NR :: 2015/16 h19s* h20g* May 15

Virgilio has already won twice early in the season, but it's not a case of missing the boat because those wins look sure to be just the precursor to further success when he returns to action after a summer break. In hindsight, odds of 7/2 for his British debut in a handicap hurdle at Warwick in May were made to look very generous as Virgilio left his French form miles behind in winning easing down by a dozen lengths from

Handazan. That came after a lengthy absence, but connections were understandably keen to turn Virgilio out quickly under a penalty after that impressive win, and six days later he was a well-backed winner of a stronger race at Aintree when readily accounting for the smart Sea Lord by six lengths. The runner-up went on to win a good-quality handicap at Market Rasen in July.

Virgilio had four starts in France for Etienne Leenders in the second half of 2013, winning over hurdles on his second outing but showing just fair form at best. His final start in France came over fences at Pau where he finished fourth, so the option of going for novice chases is open to Virgilio and he would be an exciting prospect in that sphere. But that might be jumping the gun because the best is almost certainly yet to be seen of Virgilio over hurdles first, even though he'll be running off a much higher handicap mark in future.

Sharing his sire, Denham Red, with top-class two-mile chaser Un de Sceaux, Virgilio stays two and a half miles but travels strongly and could prove just as effective at shorter. He acts on soft ground and has been tongue tied for both his starts in Britain. **Dan Skelton**

Conclusion: *Made an immediate impact in Britain, gaining quick double over hurdles in May to prove well ahead of his mark, and there's even better to come*

Volnay de Thaix (Fr) h159
6 ch.g. Secret Singer (Fr) – Mange de Thaix (Fr) (Mont Basile (Fr))
2014/15 h20.5s* h24v⁴ h20.5s² h21g⁵ h20g³ Apr 9

With Sprinter Sacre and Bobs Worth not the forces of old, Simonsig missing since the 2013 Cheltenham Festival and the pick of last season's crop of novices, Josses Hill, not hitting the heights predicted, Nicky Henderson could do with a new top-class chaser. Step forward Volnay de Thaix who has shown form on the cusp of high class over hurdles and, as a tall, useful-looking gelding, looks the type to make the grade over fences.

A useful novice hurdler in 2013/14, Volnay de Thaix made a successful return in a handicap (mark of 144) at Huntingdon last November when he easily beat Conquisto by three and a quarter lengths. Volnay de Thaix wasn't discredited on his next two starts, barely staying three miles on heavy ground when fourth to Aubusson in the valuable "Fixed Brush" Handicap at Haydock and then second of four to Rock On Ruby in the Grade 2 Relkeel at Cheltenham. A mark of 158 meant he had to carry top weight in the Coral Cup at Cheltenham next time out, and Volnay de Thaix's fifth-placed finish there was highly commendable, not least as he met some trouble. He was back in graded company for his final outing of the season, ridden too aggressively when fourteen and a half lengths third of six to Jezki in the Aintree Hurdle.

Provided Volnay de Thaix gets off to a good start over fences, the Grade 1 Scilly Isles Novices' Chase over two and a half miles at Sandown in February may be used as a stepping stone to the big spring festivals given his yard has won three of the last six renewals, including with the same owner's Punchestowns in 2010. Volnay de Thaix acts on heavy ground, though he's certainly not reliant on testing conditions. **Nicky Henderson**

Conclusion: *Very smart hurdler who has chaser written all over him; may prove best short of 3m and looks one for the JLT at the Cheltenham Festival, possibly taking in the Scilly Isles along the way*

Wait For Me (Fr) ★ b119

5 b.g. Saint des Saints (Fr) – Aulne River (Fr) (River Mist (USA))
2014/15 b16s* b16.5g³ Mar 11

Andrew Cohen has enjoyed some notable successes in National Hunt racing down the years, including with Suny Bay, who won the 1997 Hennessy and was runner-up in two Grand Nationals—the second time under 12-0, one of the great weight-carrying performances in the National—and Quinz, who landed the 2011 Racing Post Chase as a second-season novice. Quinz was trained by Philip Hobbs who looks to have another top jumping prospect for Cohen on his hands in the shape of Wait For Me.

Wait For Me made his debut in a bumper at Ascot in mid-February that has a habit of throwing up good horses, none more so than Sprinter Sacre who made his own successful introduction in the 2010 renewal. Though the latest running was rather spoilt by a slow gallop, there was no doubting Wait For Me's superiority as he led early in the straight and quickened clear to win cosily by five lengths. Wait For Me looked a live contender for the Champion Bumper at Cheltenham the following month, which his yard had won with another French-bred, Cheltenian, in 2011. Wait For Me was a 9/1-shot on the day and ran very well as he finished three lengths third of twenty-three to Moon Racer, travelling comfortably for most of the race before making his challenge over a furlong out and keeping on. It was a performance that suggested Wait For Me has the potential to become a leading novice hurdler in the new season. The robust Wait For Me has plenty of speed and can win good hurdle races over two miles, though he's bred to stay further as a half-brother to French hurdles/chase winner at up to two and a half miles Yoneti and eighteen-furlong bumper winner Welluptoscratch. He's one to look forward to over jumps. **Philip Hobbs**

Conclusion: *Showed smart form in bumpers (third to Moon Racer at the Cheltenham Festival) and has the potential to develop into a leading novice hurdler, be it over 2m or further*

Wait For Me has the potential to develop into a leading novice hurdler this season

Welsh Shadow (Ire)   b99+
5 b.g. Robin des Champs (Fr) – What A Mewsment (Ire) (Persian Mews)
2014/15 b16.5g* Mar 17

The more high-profile William Henry is still to come—for those reading A-Z at least—but in Welsh Shadow owner Dai Walters has another five-year-old with the potential to make a name for himself as a novice hurdler this season. Welsh Shadow looked a really good prospect when making a winning debut in bumpers at Wetherby in March and is in excellent hands to build on that promise. Reportedly considered a three-mile chaser in the making by his trainer Dan Skelton, Welsh Shadow can win races over hurdles first, and possibly good ones judged on the manner of his opening success.

There were some good yards/pedigrees on show among the fourteen runners for the aforementioned bumper, and they included Welsh Shadow, who was backed into joint-favouritism. Welsh Shadow raced in mid-division, went on the bridle for a long way and made good progress over three furlongs out before leading approaching the final furlong. He forged clear from there to score by seven lengths from Dueling Banjos. It looked a reasonable race of its type and the form was given some substance when the third home, Younevercall, improved to win a similar race at Southwell. In addition to such promise on the track, Welsh Shadow has a cracking jumping pedigree; he's a half-brother to fairly useful hurdler/useful chaser Klepht (winner at up to two and three quarter miles) and useful hurdler Captain Kirkton (nineteen-furlong winner), whilst his dam is a full sister to top-class chaser Celestial Gold and high-class hurdler Fiveforthree, both of whom stayed three miles. **Dan Skelton**

Conclusion: *Won by seven lengths on his bumper debut and has a top jumping pedigree (bred to stay 2¼m+); well regarded by a trainer who's made an equally impressive start to his own career*

Which One Is Which — b98p
4 b.f King's Theatre (Ire) – Presenting Copper (Ire) (Presenting)
2014/15 NR :: 2015/16 b15.8g* Jun 11

The fact that there's over eight thousand horses in training over jumps in Britain means it's rare that we have two siblings as members of the same season's *Fifty*. We have bucked the trend this time around, however, with bumper winners Which One Is Which and the year-older Copper Kay, who have both made the final cut as good prospects for the novice hurdling ranks; the pair are actually closely related, with their respective sires, King's Theatre and Kayf Tara, both sons of Sadler's Wells. Which One Is Which made a successful debut in a seven-runner mares' event at Uttoxeter in mid-June, when she led on the bridle two furlongs out to win by fourteen lengths from Midnight Gem. It looked a decent bumper on paper beforehand, featuring a nice mixture of newcomers and those already with experience, and it produced an above-average winning performance from Which One Is Which. She can win another bumper but we're really looking forward to seeing her over hurdles—she's open to considerable progress and can win decent races over timber, especially if kept to her own sex. **Jonjo O'Neill**

Conclusion: *Closely related to Copper Kay and very impressive when successful on her sole start to date in a bumper in June; will win races over hurdles, with connections having the option of keeping her to races restricted to her own sex*

William Henry (Ire) — b119+
5 b.g. King's Theatre (Ire) – Cincuenta (Ire) (Bob Back (USA))
2014/15 b16s⁴ b16g* b16m* Apr 18

In April, Nicky Henderson landed the bumper which closes Ayr's Scottish Grand National meeting for the fourth time in six years when William Henry followed in the hoofprints of Sprinter Sacre (2010), Fourth Estate (2011) and River Maigue (2012). That was William Henry's second easy win from three starts and he looks a smart prospect for novice hurdles.

William Henry came on plenty for his debut fourth at Wincanton when winning at Kempton in March by seventeen lengths, and he improved again when following up in what is invariably a good-quality race at Ayr. William Henry looked something out of the ordinary as he beat two other previous winners Sir Will and Oscar Blue by eight lengths and five lengths, tracking the pace travelling strongly before being produced to lead over two furlongs out by Nico de Boinville. The good-topped William Henry is certainly bred to do well over jumps: he's a brother to useful hurdler Sesenta (winner between two miles and two and a half miles) out of a half-sister to smart hurdler Strangely Brown (stayed three miles). William Henry was behind only OK Corral in the list of highest-rated bumper horses at Seven Barrows last term and he could well develop into the yard's best contender for next spring's Supreme Novices' Hurdle, a race in which it has saddled eight horses (including the aforementioned Sprinter Sacre) to finish in the frame in the last six renewals. **Nicky Henderson**

Conclusion: *Won twice in bumpers by wide margins, including a race won by the same yard's Sprinter Sacre, and looks a smart prospect for novice hurdles (brother to useful 2m-2½m hurdler Sesenta)*

Winner Massagot (Fr)   h133p

4 ch.g. Muhaymin (USA) – Winnor (Fr) (Lesotho (USA))
2014/15 h16.5v⁵ h16.5d h16d* h17g^F Apr 9

Alan King has won the Anniversary 4-Y-O Juvenile Hurdle at Aintree a record four times and, while he wasn't successful last season, that Winner Massagot was his sole representative says plenty about the ex-French gelding's prospects. Winner Massagot wouldn't have troubled the principals had he not fallen heavily at the final flight, but he looks just the sort who will do well in handicaps over timber in his second season, when he'll start out from what looks a very lenient BHA mark of 123. Bred for the Flat, Winner Massagot won a maiden over fourteen and a half furlongs at Royan on his only outing in France prior to switching to Barbury Castle Stables. He needed a couple of runs to get to grips with jumping but bolted up on his third start over hurdles in a two-mile maiden on good to soft ground at Kempton in late-March, unsurprisingly looking suited by the test of speed as he beat Argot by four lengths. Winner Massagot ultimately wasn't up to Grade 1 company on his final start but was set to show useful form before his final-flight departure. He's one to follow in two-mile handicaps. **Alan King**

Conclusion: *Fast-tracked from maiden hurdle win to Grade 1 company last term and can make his mark in 2m handicaps from what looks a favourable mark (123)*

Zeroeshadesofgrey (Ire) h142

6 gr.g. Portrait Gallery (Ire) – Hazy Rose (Ire) (Roselier (Fr))
2014/15 h20.5v* h24v* h24.5d* h20.5d³ h24.5d³ h24.5g[pu] Apr 10

Bred as he is, things are pretty black and white where this grey's stamina is concerned, Zeroeshadesofgrey's breeding being that of a confirmed out-and-out stayer. That being the case, it was really encouraging for his prospects as a jumper that he was able to win twice in bumpers (earning him a place in the Champion Bumper field at the 2013 Cheltenham Festival), and he duly went on to show useful form in novice hurdles in 2014/15 which really brought his stamina into play. Zeroeshadesofgrey won each of his first three starts over hurdles by wide margins at odds on, successful twice at Uttoxeter before another demolition job at Doncaster where he had more than thirty lengths to spare. The pick of his subsequent efforts in defeat was a close third behind the smart pair Caracci Apache and Blaklion in the Grade 2 River Don Novices' Hurdle back at Doncaster in January. His season ended on a low note when pulled up in the Sefton Novices' Hurdle at Aintree, but that shouldn't be allowed to overshadow the promise of his earlier efforts.

A switch to fences will give Zeroeshadesofgrey opportunities to tackle distances in excess of three miles, which should enable him to really come into his own. Roselier, the sire of his dam, was responsible for Grand National winners Royal Athlete and Bindaree among any number of good staying chasers, while his sire Portrait Gallery's best horses include the Eider winner Portrait King. Both Roselier and Portrait Gallery, incidentally, were greys. Zeroeshadesofgrey's own brother Sentimental Journey won at three and a half miles over fences, while he's very much built for chasing too, being a big, workmanlike gelding. He acts on heavy ground and tends to travel powerfully through his races. **Neil King**

Conclusion: *Useful staying novice over hurdles but a chaser in the making and bred to relish the greater tests of stamina afforded by switch to fences*

HORSES TO FOLLOW FROM IRELAND | 49

SECTION 2

DICOSIMO (FR)	50
DOUVAN (FR)	50
EMPIRE OF DIRT (IRE)	52
GALLANT OSCAR (IRE)	53
HEATHFIELD (IRE)	54
MORNING RUN (IRE)	55
NO MORE HEROES (IRE)	55
PLEASANT COMPANY (IRE)	56
SIZING JOHN	57
YORKHILL (IRE)	58

HORSES TO FOLLOW FROM IRELAND

Dicosimo (Fr)   h139

4 b.g. Laveron – Coralisse Royale (Fr) (Tip Moss (Fr))
2014/15 h16.4g^F h17.4s* h16v* h17d h16v⁴ Apr 6

The ex-French Dicosimo was ultimately disappointing on his two starts in graded company after making a winning debut for the Willie Mullins yard last January, but it's still early days with him and he can get his career right back on the up this term. There are two big factors that could see improvement from Dicosimo in the coming months: the switch to chasing and a step up beyond seventeen furlongs.

Dicosimo—who takes his name from the Italian Renaissance painter Piero di Cosimo—had two outings over timber in France for Arnaud Chaillé-Chaillé, holding every chance before falling two out on his debut at Bordeaux prior to winning a juvenile at Auteuil (wore a hood) last October. Dicosimo shaped like a horse who'd stay two and a half miles when he landed the odds in a heavy-ground juvenile at Gowran by seven and a half lengths on his debut for Mullins, dismissing his two main market rivals Prussian Eagle and Thunder Zone (who both went on to be placed at Grade 1 level) in the manner of one capable of mixing it at a higher level. Dicosimo actually shaped much better than his finishing position of eighth of sixteen suggests in the Triumph Hurdle, possibly doing a bit too much too soon as he led between the last two flights (hit 2/1-on in running on Betfair) before folding. He ran as if not fully over those exertions when a below-par fourth in the Tayto Hurdle at Fairyhouse on his final start.

Bred to jump fences, Dicosimo can hopefully follow a similar career path to the same connections' Gold Cup runner-up Djakadam (rated 134 as a juvenile hurdler) who won his first two chase starts (including the Grade 2 Killiney Novices' at Leopardstown) before falling when going well in the JLT Novices' Chase at the 2014 Cheltenham Festival. **Willie Mullins**

Conclusion: *Useful juvenile hurdler who could step up to the next level as a novice chaser; should stay 2½m+*

Douvan (Fr)   h168p

5 b.g. Walk In The Park (Ire) – Star Face (Fr) (Saint des Saints (Fr))
2014/15 h15.9g² h16.9s* h16v* h16v* h16.5g* :: 2015/16 h16d* Apr 28

Ok, so we haven't dug down too deep in the soil for this one, rather pruned him from the peak of a prized potted plant, but the main priority when compiling *Horses To Follow* is to find horses that will win races and Douvan doesn't look like getting beaten any time soon. Supreme Novices' Hurdle winner Douvan could remain over hurdles in the new season, and he's already right on the tail of the same connections' Faugheen on Timeform ratings and as low as 5/1 for the Champion Hurdle, but the

HORSES TO FOLLOW FROM IRELAND

Douvan looks another star for Willie Mullins

vibes suggest he's going chasing and it will likely take an extremely good horse—or maybe something else—to stop him blooming again back at the Cheltenham Festival in the Arkle (or even the JLT) provided all goes well.

Douvan has carried all before him since he was second on his debut in France in May 2014, winning his next start in that country before going four from four for the Mullins yard. Douvan looked very good as he beat Alpha des Obeaux by three and three quarter lengths in the Grade 2 Moscow Flyer Novices' Hurdle at Punchestown in January and outstanding when he had four and a half lengths to spare over stablemate Shaneshill in the Supreme Novices' Hurdle at Cheltenham. Douvan easily landed odds of 6/1-on on his final start in the Champion Novices' Hurdle back at Punchestown, jumping impeccably (in fact, few hurdlers in recent times have looked as quick over their hurdles) and asserting on the bridle from the last as he defeated Sizing John for the third time. Douvan really does look out of the top drawer, and as a good-topped sort he has the physique to make a chaser; "I can't wait to see him go over fences" said Willie Mullins, who sent both Champagne Fever and Vautour straight over fences in the season after their victories in the Supreme. Douvan is a strong traveller who's raced around two miles, but that's not to say he won't stay further. **Willie Mullins**

Conclusion: *Top class as a novice hurdler and hasn't finished improving yet; a clash with the same connections' Champion Hurdler Faugheen would be mouth-*

watering but looks set to switch to chasing and can prove as dominant in that sphere; deservedly ante-post favourite for the Arkle

Empire of Dirt (Ire)   c138p

8 b.g. Westerner – Rose of Inchiquin (Ire) (Roselier (Fr))
2014/15 c16s⁴ c18sF c20s³ c20v² c22vF c20v* c29vF Apr 6

Names can often belie potential just as much as they engender a sense of it. Take Empire of Dirt as a case in point. The phrase was coined to reflect a nation or kingdom with major pretensions of power but little in the way of actual prowess; essentially an illusion of strength. The Colm Murphy-trained eight-year-old who carries the same moniker may have won only one of his seven starts in an up-and-down—quite literally—first season over fences last term, but there was plenty of substance all the same, his win coming in a strong-looking novice handicap, and we are confident he can taste further success in good handicap company in 2015/16.

Owned by the powerful Gigginstown House Stud, Empire of Dirt landed two of his eight starts over hurdles in the 2013/14 campaign—which was effectively his first season of racing having made the track only once previously, in a Fairyhouse bumper in January 2012. The latter of those wins came at listed level and he also posted several useful efforts in defeat, including when runner-up to Faugheen in a novice at Navan. A chaser on looks, Empire of Dirt's progress over fences in the latest season was stop-start, with three falls on his record, the second of which denied him certain victory in a handicap at Thurles in January, five lengths up and still on the bridle at the time. He quickly made amends in the quite valuable Woodlands 100 Club Novice Handicap over two and a half miles at Naas the following month, matching the pick of his hurdling form—and producing a fluent round of jumping—when beating Champagne James by a length. Empire of Dirt was well backed upped markedly in trip in the Irish Grand National on his final outing but got no further than the first.

Empire of Dirt's jumping frailties clearly need ironing out—and it's likely his trainer will have subjected him to plenty of schooling in the close season—but the promise and form of his Naas win suggests he's well worth following in handicaps in his second season, which he starts from what looks a very attractive Irish handicap mark of 132. A prominent racer who is bred to stay three miles, Empire of Dirt acts on heavy going.
Colm Murphy

Conclusion: *Jumping problems marred his first season over fences but progressive all the same, with the highlight a win in a strong-looking novice handicap at Naas; bred to stay 3m and one to note for good-class handicaps over fences this season*

HORSES TO FOLLOW FROM IRELAND | 53

Gallant Oscar (Ire) c151p
9 b.g. Oscar (Ire) – Park Wave (Ire) (Supreme Leader)
2014/15 h23s* h23s² h20s² c25v⁴ c25g³ :: 2015/16 c25s* May 2

There aren't many nine-year-olds who have a 'p' symbol still attached to their Timeform rating, but it looks more than justified in the case of Gallant Oscar, who's had just eight starts over fences and won three of them, with his best performance coming on his latest outing. Gallant Oscar was bought privately by J. P. McManus in the week leading up to the Scottish National and was well supported for that race only to miss it amid concerns over drying ground (despite the fact he'd finished third in a big field on good ground at the latest Cheltenham Festival). The gelding still provided McManus with an instant return on his investment when winning a valuable big-field handicap chase at Punchestown's flagship meeting in May. The very well-backed Gallant Oscar cruised home with nine lengths to spare over his nearest pursuer in the style of a high-class prospect. With long distances likely to be within his compass, Gallant Oscar is worth a long-range investment for the 2016 Grand National at current odds of 33/1.

Gallant Oscar has finished in the frame on each of his nine completed starts since he joined the Tony Martin yard ahead of the 2013/14 season. He took advantage of a much lower hurdles mark when winning a Navan handicap on his return last October before finishing second in two similar events. Gallant Oscar then reverted back to chasing and made the frame in two very competitive handicaps, finishing fourth to

Gallant Oscar is a staying chaser to follow

Djakadam in the Thyestes Chase at Gowran and third to The Druids Nephew in the twenty-five furlong event on the opening day of the Cheltenham Festival. He returned two months later to beat eighteen rivals, headed by Archie Meade, at Punchestown, jumping soundly in the main and in command soon after being produced to lead between the last two fences. Stamina was at a premium at Punchestown in a well-run race on soft ground, which clearly suited Gallant Oscar. He's one to keep on side in staying events for his shrewd yard this season. **Tony Martin**

Conclusion: *Nine-year-old who was better than ever when winning valuable handicap chase at the Punchestown Festival and remains capable of even better; has done well in competitive handicaps and will stay long distances, so worth an ante-post interest for the 2016 Grand National*

Heathfield (Ire) c134p

8 ch.g. Definite Article – Famous Lady (Ire) (Presenting)
2014/15 c20.5d⁵ c22.5v* h24v² c21s² c24v* :: 2015/16 c30s* May 2

The fact they are currently betting 25/1 for the Grand National shows how difficult it is to pinpoint legitimate contenders for the world's most famous steeplechase this far in advance, but we have hopefully identified two horses in this section with more persuasive credentials than most in Gallant Oscar and Heathfield—both trained by Tony Martin for J. P. McManus—who both looked staying chasers going places when winning on the final day of the Irish season at Punchestown. Heathfield has reaped the benefit of his trainer's patient approach, proving most progressive in the latest Irish season with three wins and two seconds from six outings, and he produced a clear career-best effort on his final start when seemingly relishing the emphasis on stamina (soft ground) as he won a competitive-looking three-and-three-quarter mile handicap chase at the Punchestown Festival in great style. The most notable aspect about Heathfield's performance at Punchestown was the way he travelled—he really could be called the winner from some way out—and that suggests that not only will he be able to hold his own in a higher calibre of race, but he may be able to stay a step ahead of the handicapper for a while yet. The Grand National looks a potential long-term target for Heathfield, but his proven ability to handle very testing ground means that he's likely to be a major force in other staying handicap chases over the winter. He could hardly be in better hands, with Tony Martin having long-since proven his credentials for successfully targeting the big prizes. **Tony Martin**

Conclusion: *Progressive stayer over fences who was very impressive when landing quite valuable handicap over 3¾m at the Punchestown Festival; one to follow in similar events, and could be a potential Grand National candidate next spring*

Morning Run (Ire)   h145p
6 b.m. King's Theatre (Ire) – Portryan Native (Ire) (Be My Native (USA))
2014/15 b17d* b16m* b16g* h16d* h16g* h18v* Jan 31

Willie Mullins probably has more horses in his stable with a flawless record than most other trainers, but that shouldn't devalue the remarkable consistency of a horse like Morning Run, who was last seen extending her winning sequence to six with a smart effort in the Grade 3 Solerina Mares Novices' Hurdle at Fairyhouse in January. Morning Run—who started her career in bumpers last May—was undoubtedly stylish in her three wins over hurdles last season, but her form is not devoid of substance, either, with those playing second fiddle to her including the likes of subsequent Grade 3 winner Carrigmoorna Rock and stable-companion Lyrical Theatre, another highly-promising mare who went on to be placed in Grade 1 company in the spring. Although it is slightly concerning that we didn't see Morning Run at any of the big spring meetings, for which her entries had included the championship novice races, the strong impression she made over the winter means she definitely deserves a place in this section. Although her yard also have the likes of Annie Power and Vroum Vroum Mag to think about, she could well end up a leading contender for the David Nicholson Mares' Hurdles at the Cheltenham Festival, a race her yard have monopolised since its inception in 2008. A half-sister by King's Theatre to the useful hurdler/chaser Morning Supreme, who stayed two and a half miles, Morning Run will have little trouble staying beyond two and a quarter miles. **Willie Mullins**

Conclusion: *Unbeaten in six starts, including three over hurdles, and will continue as a leading contender for mares' graded events, possibly including the Mares' Hurdle at Cheltenham (likely to stay 2½m)*

No More Heroes (Ire)   h153
6 br.g. Presenting – What A Breeze (Ire) (Naheez (USA))
2014/15 h22s* h20s* h20s⁵ h24d³ :: 2015/16 h24s⁵ Apr 29

A thirty-nine length success in a Leopardstown bumper in the 2013/14 season led to No More Heroes being one of the most well-touted novice hurdlers in Gordon Elliott's yard last year, and he looks an equally good prospect for chasing ahead of this season. No More Heroes didn't disappoint his supporters early on over timber, landing a maiden at Punchestown on his hurdling debut in November and then turning over the Champion Bumper runner-up Shaneshill in the Grade 2 Navan Novices' Hurdle. A bad scope was to blame for No More Heroes' below-par effort in another Grade 2 novice next time out at Leopardstown. Runner-up that day was Martello Tower, who came out on top against No More Heroes once more when winning the Albert Bartlett at the Cheltenham Festival. No More Heroes was right back on his game that day though in finishing a close third, and he was arguably unlucky not to win, having been denied a clear run and lost momentum before the final flight. He clearly wasn't himself when only fifth behind Killultagh Vic in the equivalent event at Punchestown six weeks later.

As a winning pointer who quickly reached a very smart level over hurdles, No More Heroes looks a cracking novice chase prospect. The Albert Bartlett has proven to be a useful stepping stone for many future staying chasers, with recent winners Bobs Worth and Weapon's Amnesty returning to Cheltenham to win the following year's RSA Chase, so it is no surprise to see No More Heroes, arguably the best chasing prospect of the front three in last year's Albert Bartlett, at the head of most ante-post markets for this season's RSA. He's one to follow over fences. **Gordon Elliott**

Conclusion: *Very smart novice hurdle form, and arguably shaped best when close third in the Albert Bartlett; has looked a staying chaser in the making for some time and likely to take high rank in the novice division this term*

Pleasant Company (Ire) h131
7 b.g. Presenting – Katie Flame (Ire) (Alderbrook)
2014/15 h22s⁴ h24d³ :: 2015/16 h24d³ h20s⁴ May 2

With six straight defeats—four of them as favourite—since a successful debut under Rules in a bumper back in November 2013, Pleasant Company has undoubtedly been an expensive horse to follow hitherto. Such a run is even more surprising considering he's been housed in two of the most powerful stables on either side of the Irish Sea, having started out under the care of David Pipe before switching to Willie Mullins after his reappearance in the latest season. Pleasant Company's three runs since relocated to Ireland have been brimming with promise, however, and we are banking that he can repay his supporters faith in handicaps this term.

Pleasant Company's debut success at Ascot was followed by a couple of subdued-but-explicable runs over hurdles, but a flop in a tongue tie back at Ascot on his reappearance in the latest season led to a change of scenery (the gelding remains in the colours of Malcolm Denmark). It was to be five months before Pleasant Company made his debut for Mullins. When he did, he was backed as though defeat was out of the question on his handicap bow at the Irish Grand National meeting. It evidently wasn't as he could finish only third, though the first three pulled well clear and he'd been worst-placed of them, beaten only two necks nonetheless. He also suffered the ignominy of twice being a beaten favourite at the same Punchestown Festival, though both failures can be explained away, especially the second occasion when he did well to keep on for fourth after conceding first run to the principals. A tall point-winner, Pleasant Company is bound for fences in due course, but there are handicaps to be won with him over hurdles first. He's raced only on ground softer than good (acts on soft). **Willie Mullins**

Conclusion: *Unexposed hurdler who has shaped like a winner in waiting on all three starts since joining Willie Mullins; can win a handicap or two before switching to fences; stays 3m but at least as effective over 2½m*

Sizing John   h153
5 b.g. Midnight Legend – La Perrotine (Fr) (Northern Crystal)
2014/15 b16g⁴ h16d* h16v² h16s* h16.5g³ :: 2015/16 16d² Apr 28

That clichéd saying involving words such as 'whatever', 'hurdles' and 'bonus' is one of those racing proverbs which does hold plenty of truth for many of Henry de Bromhead's horses, who quite often enjoy their better days once they have made the switch from hurdles to fences. As far as bonuses over hurdles go, then, Sizing John's victory in the Grade 1 Future Champions Novices' Hurdle at Leopardstown in December was a fairly lucrative one. When you consider that win was his trainer's first Grade 1 success over timber since 2008, when the yard's subsequent top-class chaser Sizing Europe won the Irish Champion Hurdle, then the excitement at the prospect of Sizing John transferring to fences this season is only heightened.

Although the Future Champions Novices' represented the only victory over hurdles for Sizing John besides his maiden win at Naas last season, it didn't signify his peak, and we may have even been talking about Sizing John as a dual-Grade 1-winning hurdler if it wasn't for Willie Mullins' star novice Douvan, who was ahead of him on three occasions throughout the season, including on Sizing John's final start when the pair finished first and second—separated by seven and a half lengths—in the Champion Novices' Hurdle at the Punchestown Festival. Sizing John had finished marginally closer to Douvan when third in the Supreme at Cheltenham on his previous outing, an effort which represented a hefty chunk of improvement on the part of Sizing John on his first outing since the aforementioned Leopardstown win. Given his promise as an embryonic chaser, the feeling is that the switch to fences will only bring Sizing John closer to Douvan. The two are not necessarily guaranteed to meet this season, though, with a step up to beyond two miles very much likely to suit Sizing John. Either way, he looks a very exciting recruit to the novice chasing ranks. **Henry de Bromhead**

Conclusion: *Smart, Grade 1-winning novice hurdler last term, when also running with plenty of credit behind Douvan at Cheltenham and Punchestown; a chaser in the making and will do well in the novice division this season; will stay beyond 2m*

 Download the App!

Yorkhill (Ire) b125p

5 ch.g. Presenting – Lightning Breeze (Ire) (Saddlers' Hall (Ire))
2014/15 b18v* :: 2015/16 b16g* Apr 30

Briar Hill, Shaneshill, Bellshill; and now Yorkhill. Each began his career in Irish points for trainer Colin McKeever and owner Wilson Dennison before joining Willie Mullins and running in the colours of Andrea and Graham Wylie. Bellshill and Yorkhill, who were both bought as foals by Ian Ferguson (who trained Simonsig in points) and named after areas in Scotland, were first and second in the list of Timeform's highest-rated bumper performers in Britain and Ireland in 2014/15. It was tough to decide which of the pair to side with for this list, and it's the more lightly-raced (and unbeaten) profile of Yorkhill which just tipped the balance in his favour. Yorkhill is a very exciting prospect for novice hurdles and it will be disappointing if he doesn't develop into a major player for one of the Grade 1 novice events at the Cheltenham Festival, with his stamina-laden pedigree suggesting the three-mile Albert Bartlett could be the race for him.

Yorkhill won his completed start between the flags over three miles and is out of a close relation to the smart chaser at up to three miles Dooneys Gate (trained by Willie Mullins), who's also a half-sister to top-class staying chaser The Listener. It was no surprise, therefore, that he relished the good test over eighteen furlongs on heavy ground when making his Rules debut at Gowran in March (four days before the Champion Bumper at Cheltenham), landing the odds by two and three quarter lengths from Pause And Ponder, with the pair well clear. Yorkhill was sent off 5/4 favourite for his subsequent outing at Punchestown, despite dropping back in trip and facing six other winners in an eight-runner field, among them the once-raced pair Newsworthy and OK Corral from the Nicky Henderson yard. Yorkhill showed much improved form to follow up in most taking fashion as he and OK Corral pulled well clear of the rest, producing a level of performance that would have seen him go close in any of the championship events at the major spring festivals. The turn of foot Yorkhill showed to put the race to bed on the home turn was all the more impressive given his breeding. As ever, the Willie Mullins yard will have a raft of quality novice hurdlers this season—and one has already started, Bachasson winning all three of his hurdling starts between July and September and as low as 7/1 for the Supreme Novices' at the time of writing—and Yorkhill has the potential to prove as good as any of them. **Willie Mullins**

Conclusion: *Behind only the same connections' Bellshill among the top bumper performers last season when he won both his starts, defeating Fifty member OK Corral at Punchestown; looks as good a prospect as there is for novice hurdles*

LOOKING AHEAD

SECTION 3

TALKING TO THE TRAINERS	60
Paul Nicholls	60
Nicky Henderson	60
Philip Hobbs	61
Willie Mullins	62
David Pipe	62
Oliver Sherwood	63
Jonjo O'Neill	63
Dan Skelton	64
Warren Greatrex	64
Harry Fry	65
RISING STARS	66
Ben Pauling	66
Henry Oliver	67
David Mullins	68
Jack Kennedy	69
ANTE-POST BETTING	71
WHAT'S THE POINT?	78

HORSES TO FOLLOW

TALKING TO THE TRAINERS

To give some pointers for the new season, we asked a number of leading National Hunt trainers to pick out a star performer, handicapper and dark horse to follow from their respective stables. Read on to find out what names came back...

Paul Nicholls

Position in 2014/15 Trainers' Championship	1st
Wins-Runs in Britain in 2014/15	124/517
Highest-rated horse in training	Silviniaco Conti Timeform Rating c172

Star Performer Silviniaco Conti 'He keeps on winning and there's plenty still to come from him. Another crack at the Gold Cup seems very unlikely unless he were to show improved form. I suspect we'll aim Betfair Chase, King George and then some races in Ireland or perhaps the Aintree race (Bowl, which he's won for the last two years). It's possible that he'll have a prep again before the Betfair—he might go to Down Royal if we can get him ready in time; he's just taken a little while to come to hand, that's all.'

Handicapper Monsieur Gibraltar (h138p) 'He's a horse I think will do well in handicaps this season; though hopefully he'll be one of a number to do so. He's an ex-French horse who won on his only start for us at Newton Abbot. He's a really nice type of horse and I think he'll progress really nicely.'

Dark Horse Boa Island (b79) 'He ran in a bumper last October for Stuart Crawford and then won two point-to-points for Jack Barber in the spring. He's a nice, big, backward horse who'll have a run in an amateur riders' novice hurdle at Exeter in October and then go chasing. He's one to keep an eye on.'

Nicky Henderson

Position in 2014/15 Trainers' Championship	2nd
Wins-Runs in Britain in 2014/15	129/499
Highest-rated horse in training	My Tent Or Yours Timeform Rating h168

Star Performer Peace And Co (h161P) 'He's had a good summer. It's notoriously difficult for the four- and five-year-olds to step up to highest level, but we have to hope

TALKING TO THE TRAINERS | 61

he's a Champion Hurdle horse—if he isn't he'll struggle, and that's the same every year with the Triumph Hurdle winner. The record of five-year-olds in the Champion Hurdle isn't great, but we can always break that rule. As for specific races, we'll have to juggle him around with My Tent Or Yours, who's back in training; you'd hope they'd be the two for the Champion Hurdle, though we've also got Top Notch and Hargam.'

Handicapper Cocktails At Dawn (c145) 'I let him win his novice at Sandown on his final start last season, and he'll go novice chasing while he still can (until October) before having a crack at the Paddy Power Gold Cup at Cheltenham or something like that.'

Dark Horse Altior (b115) 'Lessons In Milan could be one for novice chasing, but I'm going to say Altior again—I know I gave him to you as my 'Dark Horse' last year but I messed it up a bit and he stayed in bumpers. He'll go novice hurdling this time around and will be very good.'

Philip Hobbs

Position in 2014/15 Trainers' Championship	3rd
Wins-Runs in Britain in 2014/15	102/551
Highest-rated horse in training	Menorah Timeform Rating c169

Star Performer Wait for Me (b118) 'He won easily on his debut in an Ascot bumper and ran a fantastic race to be third in the Cheltenham Festival bumper. He'll start over hurdles in late-October.'

Handicapper Sausalito Sunrise (c143+) 'He won his first chase followed by two seconds at Cheltenham (beaten by Kings Palace both times). He could well be capable of winning a decent handicap this season.'

Dark Horse Dalia Pour Moi (b-) 'He ran three times in Ireland, once in a bumper and twice in points, winning on his completed start, and has been bought by Highclere Thoroughbred Racing. He's pleased us in all his work and will start back in a bumper or novice hurdle in late-October.'

Follow the Fifty with My Timeform!

Add them to your tracker & get free alerts when they run

at timeform.com & on the App **TF**

TALKING TO THE TRAINERS

Willie Mullins

Position in 2014/15 Trainers' Championship	4th (Champion Trainer in Ireland)
Wins-Runs in Britain in 2014/15	16/91
Highest-rated horse in training	Vautour c171p/Faugheen h171+

Star Performer Faugheen 'He's summered very well and has come back nice and strong. He's taking his training well, though we haven't thought about the specifics of his campaign yet.'

Handicapper Urano (c143) 'He was just beaten a short head in the Kerry National in September. He looks to be improving—he's still only seven—and could be one that crosses over to England for some of the big handicaps there.'

Dark Horse Sure Reef (h138p) 'He's probably not that 'dark'—we don't tend to have 'dark' horses!—but he hasn't run since January 2014 and is a horse we like. He showed huge potential on the Flat and then showed us lots over hurdles, winning his two completed starts, including a Grade 2. He's back and in good form, and is a horse who could go the whole way to the top.'

David Pipe

Position in 2014/15 Trainers' Championship	5th
Wins-Runs in 2014/15	116/579
Highest-rated horse in training	Dynaste Timeform Rating c167

Star Performer Dynaste 'He's back from the injury that stopped him running during the second half of last season. He was a close third behind Many Clouds in the BetBright Cup at Cheltenham in January on his final start – form that is looking quite handy now with the winner subsequently landing the Grand National. He will be going for similar races again this season - the Betfair Chase at Haydock and the King George VI Chase at Kempton on Boxing Day are obvious targets, while he could well start off over in France.'

Handicapper Herbert Park (h132) 'A lovely five-year-old gelding by Shantou who did extremely well last season, winning a bumper and two hurdle races. It was encouraging that he had the speed to beat subsequent Cheltenham Festival winner Qualando over two miles, while he also demonstrated the necessary stamina to win over three miles at Kempton. He has strengthened up well over the summer and will probably start off in hurdles before going novice chasing.'

Dark Horse Eamon An Cnoic 'He was bought for €175,000 at Goffs in April of this year having finished a promising second in an Irish point-to-point at Oldcastle on his only start to date. A good looking four-year-old son of Westerner with plenty of size and scope, he will probably start off in a bumper somewhere.'

Oliver Sherwood

Position in 2014/15 Trainers' Championship	7th
Wins-Runs in Britain in 2014/15	31/204
Highest-rated horse in training	Many Clouds Timeform Rating c168

Star Performer Many Clouds 'Obviously, Many Clouds was a star for us last season. He looks great and we're looking at the Hennessy for his first big target, though I wouldn't be keen on running him with top weight, so hopefully Coneygree runs too. He could have a prep but it depends on the ground. Hopefully all roads will lead to Aintree again, though I'm still undecided as to whether to take in the Gold Cup on the way.'

Handicapper Kings Bandit (h142p, c-p) 'We've inherited him from Donald McCain and think he could be a nice novice handicap chaser this season. We think his mark of 132 is workable, and he could fly under the radar a bit given he's still lightly raced.'

Dark Horse Robinesse (b100+) 'She won at Uttoxeter on her only bumper start, and one of those that dead-heated for second won next time. She's a half-sister to our Mischievous Milly and we think she'll do well in mares' races.'

Jonjo O'Neill

Position in 2014/15 Trainers' Championship	8th
Wins-Runs in Britain in 2014/15	104/634
Highest-rated horse in training	More of That Timeform Rating h170

Star Performer Holywell (c163) 'Hopefully he will start off in the Charlie Hall at Wetherby. His races will be relatively mapped out from then – if he goes well it will be Haydock (for the Betfair Chase) and possibly the King George, ground depending, with the Gold Cup as his long-term plan.'

Handicapper Johns Spirit (c158) 'With his rating as it is now (BHA mark of 157) he will be going for the good-class races over two and a half miles.'

Dark Horse Which One Is Which (b98p) 'She won her bumper well and will be aimed at the mares' only novice hurdles this season.'

Dan Skelton

Position in 2014/15 Trainers' Championship	12th
Wins-Runs in Britain in 2014/15	73/377
Highest-rated horse in training	Blue Heron Timeform Rating h155

Star Performer Value At Risk (c146) 'He goes chasing this year and will go to Bangor at the end of October. He'll then hopefully go to the Hennessy meeting. Obviously, he was one of the leading three-mile hurdlers last season and was the first of the English home in the Albert Bartlett. We think we can get him better than he was last term as we only inherited him half-way through. We've got high aspirations for him.'

Handicapper Zarib (h130) 'He'll start off in the Elite Hurdle at Wincanton in November. We were very happy with him last season but we rode him too prominently in the Fred Winter at Cheltenham, when he was just about still leading over the last but didn't quite get home. We'll ride him a little differently and look for tracks that may suit him better, and there's a race in him off a mark of 133.'

Dark Horse Fou Et Sage (h150) 'He's a very good horse. He won a listed handicap hurdle at Auteuil that worked out well and was beaten only by Bonito du Berlais in Grade 3s on his final two starts there. He's obviously well-known in France, and we think he can become just as well-known over here this season. He'll likely return in a four-year-olds only hurdle at Cheltenham on 24th October.'

Warren Greatrex

Position in 2014/15 Trainers' Championship	18th
Wins-Runs in Britain in 2014/15	51/272
Highest-rated horse in training	Cole Harden Timeform Rating h164

Star Performer Shantou Bob (h141) 'He was just touched off in a Grade 2 last year, then finished third in a Grade 2 and sixth in the Albert Bartlett, but he was struggling with his wind all last season. He had a minor op before Cheltenham but it wasn't enough, so we gave him another operation over the summer. His work looks really good and as long as the ground looks ok he'll run in the Silver Trophy at Chepstow (10th October) before embarking on a chase career. I think on soft ground he's well up to making his presence felt in a top-grade race; he's got a real will to win and is improving all the time.'

Handicapper Missed Approach (h120) 'He'd won his point before he came to me, and he then won his bumper and his novice hurdle. I then ran him back too quickly when he was third at Wetherby, though he got beat by a really good horse called Three Musketeers who went on to win a Grade 2; we had to give 7 lb to him that day as we had a penalty. He was never quite right after that so I didn't run him, but he's come back in looking great and will stay hurdling, with his mark of 123 looking ok to go on with.'

Dark Horse Aloomomo (h104; c106p) 'He came to me quite late last season from France, and I just sort of went on what I was advised really. I ran him over three and a quarter miles at Carlisle and put cheekpieces on because they'd told me he raced lazily, and James Reveley rode him as he'd been riding him in France. He travelled very well that day and then didn't quite get home. I then ran him over hurdles as the owners wanted a runner at the Ayr meeting. He's had a good summer and we'll start from scratch. He's come in a different horse and he could just go onto better things starting from a mark of 109.'

Harry Fry

Position in 2014/15 Trainers' Championship	19th
Wins-Runs in Britain in 2014/15	36/157
Highest-rated horse in training	Rock On Ruby Timeform Rating **h163**

Star Performer Activial (h152) 'He's going novice chasing this season. Obviously, he ran in the French Champion Hurdle at the beginning of June and is just back cantering. He'll run at the end of November and will hopefully make up into a top performer in the division between two and a half miles and three miles.'

Handicapper Gunner Fifteen (h124p) 'He's joined us from Fergal O'Brien and is hopefully unexposed after just four starts. He'll be one to keep on side and will start back over hurdles.'

Dark Horse Calling des Blins 'She's a filly that we hope will be a horse to follow in juvenile races this season (won a three-year-old bumper on her only start in France).'

RISING STARS
Ben Pauling

Base	Bourton on the Water, Gloucestershire
First Full Licence	2013
First Jumps Winner	**Raven's Tower** Plumpton 04/11/13
Total Winners	29
Best Horse Trained	**Barters Hill** Timeform Rating b121+

Ben Pauling grew up around horses and always had designs on a career in racing. He spent six years as assistant trainer to Nicky Henderson before setting up on his own in 2013. Pauling enjoyed a fantastic season in 2014/15, when his twenty winners were capped by the unbeaten Barters Hill's success in the Grade 2 bumper at Aintree's Grand National meeting. Every fledgling yard needs a flagship horse like Barters Hill, who beat the subsequent Punchestown Grade 1 winner Bellshill at Aintree and was bought by Pauling as an unraced three-year-old for €16,000, but as is highlighted in 'Trainer's View', his eggs aren't just in one basket. Pauling has also done well with horses he's acquired from other yards—Malibu Sun, Smart Freddy and Ergo Sum, for example—and it says plenty that he's been sent the progressive Irish hurdler Drumacoo for the new season. Pauling also sent out Raven's Tower—who he picked up for just £2,000 from the Flat—to win three times and finish sixth in the Fred Winter as a juvenile hurdler in 2013/14.

Pauling has a great set-up at Bourton Hill Farm near Cheltenham, which is located near the yards of Jonjo O'Neill, Nigel Twiston-Davies and Charlie Longsdon. The trainer has access to a five-and-a-half-furlong polytrack gallop, indoor and outdoor schools, a spa and solarium amongst other things, and such facilities should allow the operation to continue its progress. Another key feature of the stable are the jockeys David Bass and Nico de Boinville, who both rode winners at the 2015 Cheltenham Festival. Bass and de Boinville were given plenty of opportunities as young jockeys by Nicky Henderson, and it's intriguing that Pauling has been doing similar with his yard's conditional Harrison Beswick. Ben Pauling has made a very promising start to his career as a trainer and can step up to the next level in the coming years

Trainer's View: "We'll have between forty-four and fifty horses in this season. We're very much trying to concentrate on some better quality horses, and we've tried to get rid of those that are badly handicapped or we can't see much future for. We've bought a lot of three-year-olds, privately and from the sales, and we're replenishing our bumper stock, as it were; this is something I've taken Nicky's advice on. It was the young horses that really shone for us last season.

Barters Hill was obviously a good horse for us, and we don't really know what his limits are as he's led from pillar to post in most of his races. We're looking forward to his progress this year and he'll start off in a couple of ordinary, mid-week novice hurdles. If he wins those we won't just keep carrying extra weight, we'll very much look down the graded route. He'll probably be better over two and a half miles and my first thought for him would be the Challow at Christmas time. Another horse I think a lot of is **Ballyhenry** who won his two starts in bumpers. He's a big, backward Presenting horse and right from the start we said we wouldn't be going into any championship bumpers with him, whereas Barters Hill had actually been in training the whole of the previous season without getting to the racecourse because he was too weak. Ballyhenry is an exceptionally smart horse and his jumping is by far and away his biggest asset. He'll have a similar campaign to Barters Hill. Another horse to mention from bumpers is **Always Lion** who posted some nice performances last term, including when second under a penalty to Wait For Me at Ascot when he wasn't even fully tuned up. I hugely regret running him in the Champion Bumper; he wasn't man enough for the job. He's bigger and stronger now. Finally, we've been sent **Drumacoo** from Ireland and he looks a horse who should do well having won his last three starts."

Henry Oliver

Base	Abberley, Worcestershire
First Full Licence	2013
First Jumps Winner	**Signed Request** Chepstow 06/04/13
Total Winners	37
Best Horse Trained	**Dresden** Timeform Rating c137

There can't be many people that have ridden a horse in a race and then, after retiring from the saddle, gone on to train the same horse. Henry Oliver will do just that this season as he now trains Restless Harry who he rode to win three Grade 2 events over hurdles from 2010 to 2012 when the gelding was in the care of Robin Dickin. What Oliver can do with an exposed eleven-year-old whose two runs last season suggested he might be ready for retirement remains to be seen, but he certainly caught the eye with his training exploits last term and has plenty of up-and-coming horses at his Worsley Racing Stables. Two of them are Whispering Harry and Keel Haul—both owned by Restless Harry's owner Richard Whitehead—who have been with Oliver since he started training and have won ten races between them, including four chases in 2014/15. Beatabout The Bush and Dresden became Oliver's first Cheltenham Festival runners last March and, while neither troubled the judge, they were fully entitled to be there having won their previous starts impressively. Oliver sent out two winners from fifteen runners in his first season, thirteen winners from one hundred runners in 2013/14 and twenty-one winners from one hundred and seven runners in 2014/15 (when backing all of his runners would have yielded a £400 profit to a £10 level stake). Oliver was a fair jockey—he rode two hundred and thirty-two winners during eighteen seasons in the saddle—but he could make a bigger impression as a trainer; make sure you give his horses respect this season.

David Mullins

Attached Stable	Thomas Mullins
First Ride	2012
First Winner	**Rathvawn Belle** Punchestown 20/02/2013
Total Winners	50 (including 1 on the Flat)
Best Horse Ridden	**Savello/Rule The World** Timeform Rating c152

Here we have another talented member of the Mullins family. David Mullins is son of trainer Tom Mullins (brother of Willie Mullins) and has created a very good impression in his short career as a jockey. He won on his sixth ride when guiding 33/1-shot Rathvawn Belle to score in a big-field sales bumper at Punchestown. Mullins rode eleven more winners as an amateur before switching to the conditional ranks, gaining his first win in that sphere on his father's veteran Fosters Cross last December. Mullins—who also rode a winner on the Flat (the Willie Mullins-trained Lucky Bridle) in Ireland in 2014—showcased his skills on this side of the Irish Sea eight times last season and won on two of his mounts, namely Astre de La Cour and Wicked Spice at the big meetings at Aintree and Ayr respectively. Mullins was especially impressive on Wicked Spice as the gelding went in snatches and was outpaced four furlongs out before leading on the run-in. Mullins' talents were also seen on another horse at the

Grand National fixture, the Tony Martin-trained Marinero whose saddle slipped before the second last flight. Mullins kicked his feet out of his irons and rode Marinero over the second last, and he was still there with a chance going into the final flight only for the horse to clip the top of the obstacle and fall; if the gelding hadn't come down it would have been hailed as one of the rides of the season. It was also significant that Mullins was picked by Willie Mullins to ride the favourite Roi des Francs in the Martin Pipe at the latest Cheltenham Festival, though in the event the pair could finish only third to the same stable's Killultagh Vic (who was ridden by another promising Irish conditional, Luke Dempsey). Mullins also got the job done on the smart Mouse Morris-trained chaser Real Steel when he was sent off favourite for a Punchestown handicap in May, while he also rode the same stable's Rule The World to finish third in the Kerry National at Listowel in September. Teenager David Mullins is developing a reputation for being both strong and tactically astute in the saddle, and there's no doubt he has the potential to become a top rider over the coming years

Jack Kennedy

Attached Stable	Gordon Elliott
First Ride	2015
First Winner	**Funny How** Cork 22/05/15
Total Winners	**20 (including 6 on the Flat)**
Best Horse Ridden	**Bayan** Timeform Rating h150

Further evidence of the very strong bunch of young riders in Ireland at present—and remember, Jonathan Burke was the main focus of our *Rating The Riders* feature in last season's book—comes from Jack 'J. W.' Kennedy. Kennedy had his first ride under Rules only in May but he's already looked a top prospect, something very much backed up by the unique Timeform Jockey Ratings (an impressive proportion of his rides have 'run to form'). Kennedy rode two hundred and twenty-one pony-race winners in Ireland and was champion jockey on the circuit for three years, and it's clear that has proved a good foundation as he's another teenage conditional who looks mature, both mentally and physically. Kennedy is attached to the Gordon Elliott yard and made his thoroughbred race-riding debut on the trainer's Taglietelle on the Flat at Clonmel—it was very interesting that he was entrusted to ride that gelding who'd won a big handicap hurdle at Aintree on his previous start and was a short-priced favourite (Kennedy has also been riding the yard's smart hurdler Bayan in recent months). Kennedy's first four rides all finished placed and three of them came in big fields, including on a gelding trained by the shrewd Tony Carroll in a 'hands and heels' apprentice race at Newmarket (clearly Kennedy had a good reputation from an early stage). Kennedy got off the mark on his seventh ride—just fifteen days after his first—which, as with David Mullins, came on a horse who started 33/1 in a big field. Kennedy enjoyed his first high-profile success on Clondaw Warrior in a Flat handicap at the Galway Festival which came on his first ride for Willie Mullins, and it spoke volumes that the master trainer turned again to Kennedy when Frankie Dettori switched from Wicklow Brave to Clondaw Warrior (who was initially a reserve) in the Ebor in August. Mullins' comments before the race—"We've got two good horses and two good jockeys"—were praise indeed for Kennedy, and the rider looked as good as most professionals as he drove Wicklow Brave into second place, albeit picking up a ban for using the whip above the permitted level (it is hoped that he learns from his transgression). Quite simply, Jack Kennedy looks a real talent and his 7-lb claim is a steal.

HORSES TO FOLLOW

ANTE-POST BETTING

Timeform's Features Writer John Ingles casts his eye over the markets for the feature races in the National Hunt calendar, picking out some value bets along the way…

'Machines will be capable, within twenty years, of doing any work a man can do.' The words are those of the eminent American social scientist Herbert Simon who made his bold prediction in 1956. One of the pioneers of Artificial Intelligence, Simon clearly got a lot right in his brilliant career in a number of different fields—he was a Nobel Prize winner for Economics, after all—so it does seem a bit unfair that he should have gained some sort of fame for getting something badly wrong. I'm glad he did though, on a couple of counts. For one thing, it means I still have a job, though we'll see if that's still the case after the Grand National! Secondly, it shows that predicting events some time in the future is fraught with uncertainty. So until Timeform come up with a machine to do the job, here are some ante-post selections for the season ahead…

King George VI Chase

Vautour heads the King George betting at a general 3/1 and it's hard to find fault with his record since joining Willie Mullins for whom he has won all but one of his nine starts. His only blip came at Leopardstown on Boxing Day last season when he all but fell, but his jumping was superb when winning the JLT Novices' Chase at Cheltenham on his final start where he stayed on strongly over two and a half miles. However, Vautour is a short price for one yet to tackle three miles, and if Gold Cup winner **Coneygree** lines up against him, Vautour will face another confirmed front-runner—and a proven stayer at that—who will be intent on making it a true test. Indeed, it's surprising that Coneygree is generally shorter in the King George betting than for the Gold Cup as he looked much more at home around Cheltenham's stiffer track than he did when winning the Kauto Star Novices' under less testing conditions on Boxing Day last year, a race that fell apart behind him. **Saphir du Rheu** was one of those who failed to complete behind Coneygree at Kempton, though was much more fluent when making an impressive return

ANTE-POST BETTING

Dual Betfair Chase and King George winner Silviniaco Conti

to fences in the Mildmay Novices' at Aintree in the spring. But while Saphir du Rheu still has to prove himself in open company over fences, his stable-companion **Silviniaco Conti** was as good as ever when winning his second King George last December and will surely have his season focussed on a hat-trick bid at Kempton given his three failures now in the Gold Cup. Sent off at 15/8 when winning the 2014 King George, Silviniaco Conti looks value at 6/1 to win for a third time in a race where repeat winners are common. A potentially bigger threat than Vautour from Ireland is **Don Cossack** who ended last season in style with wins at Aintree and Punchestown that made him the best chaser in training, though the Lexus Chase would be an alternative for him at home. One who appeals each way at a bigger price (25/1)—as a strong-travelling hold-up performer in a race where there should be no hanging around—is **Ballynagour** who ran Silviniaco Conti to a head in the Bowl at Aintree in April.

SELECTION Silviniaco Conti (6/1)

Champion Hurdle

If the betting for next year's Champion Hurdle is anything to go by, Willie Mullins not only has an excellent chance of winning the race again but could pull off the feat of saddling the first three once more. Dual winner Hurricane Fly might have

ANTE-POST BETTING

been retired, but last season's runner-up **Arctic Fire**, hugely impressive Supreme Novices' winner **Douvan** (probably more likely to go chasing) and another leading novice of last term **Nichols Canyon** all provide back-up to unbeaten 2015 winner **Faugheen** who is only a shade of odds against at best to win it again. That's more live Champion Hurdle hopes in one Irish stable than there are at present in the whole of Britain, but if there's one who can fill the void to become top two-mile hurdler on this side of the Irish Sea, then it's unbeaten Triumph Hurdle winner **Peace And Co**. His trainer Nicky Henderson emulated Mullins when completing a one-two-three of his own in the Triumph and has already won the Champion Hurdle five times. Peace And Co may have had only a neck to spare over runner-up **Top Notch**, but he was idling in front and if he makes the expected improvement between now and the Festival—there doesn't look to be much standing in his way among the British hurdlers—then the 10/1 currently widely available could look very big. Triumph Hurdle winners may not have the best record when graduating to open company, but Peace And Co has more physical scope than most, as well as a serious amount of ability for a four-year-old, something he showed as early as his stunning British debut at Doncaster last December.

SELECTION Peace And Co (10/1)

Peace And Co (left) challenges stablemate Top Notch at the last in the Triumph Hurdle

Queen Mother Champion Chase

The outstanding Arkle winner **Un de Sceaux** is a short price to make a winning return to the Festival in the Champion Chase, justifiably so given his electric performance against his fellow novices was already well up to Champion Chase-winning standard. 2015 winner **Dodging Bullets** is his only real rival in the ante-post betting, though he'll probably have more on his plate in a repeat bid than when beating a field that included former winners **Sire de Grugy** and **Sprinter Sacre** whose best days are almost certainly behind them. However, there are others that make more appeal as potential each-way shots at decent odds. The way **Uxizandre** took the Ryanair Chase at the latest Festival when unchallenged from the front to give Tony McCoy his final win at the meeting suggests that the Champion Chase might be considered as an alternative for him next March. In which case odds as big as 25/1 are tempting, though pulling off the same tactics against the front-running Un de Sceaux would be a tall order. The Ryanair is obviously an option for Uxizandre again, though it's worth remembering that he beat Dodging Bullets over two miles at Cheltenham last autumn. Henry de Bromhead trained a past winner of the Champion Chase in the recently retired Sizing Europe, while **Special Tiara** finished third for him in the latest renewal (before beating Sprinter Sacre at Sandown), but it's the stable's potential Champion Chase contender of the future that we're interested in. Available at 33/1 in places, Maghull Novices' winner **Sizing Granite**, unbeaten in completed starts over fences and progressing with each race, has the potential to be trading at much shorter odds by March.

SELECTIONS Sizing Granite (33/1 each-way)

World Hurdle

Here's a race without a short-priced Willie Mullins-trained favourite—though that's not to say he's lacking a leading contender. 2014 runner-up **Annie Power** may be vying for favouritism in plenty of lists but she ran in the Mares' Hurdle instead at the latest Festival and there must be a very good chance she'll go for the same race again in an attempt to atone for her last-flight fall which cost her certain victory last March. Former Champion Hurdle winner Jezki was the other heading the betting after his beating of Hurricane Fly in the World Series Hurdle over three miles at Punchestown, but he's been ruled out for the season just as this book was being put together. 2015 World Hurdle winner **Cole Harden** and **Whisper**—who beat Cole Harden into second when landing his second Liverpool Hurdle at Aintree in April—head up an open division at present, but only in the absence of the exciting

2014 winner **More of That** who, for all that he might still have more to offer, has been seen out only once since looking such a good prospect when beating Annie Power at Cheltenham. Last season's novices **Windsor Park** and **Nichols Canyon** (first and third respectively in the Neptune at the Festival) are others prominent in an open market, though both that Flat-bred pair have yet to tackle three miles. **Saphir du Rheu**'s attempt to do a 'Big Buck's' nearly came off when runner-up to Cole Harden in March, though a bid to go one better in 2016 would presumably only happen if his promising chasing career fails to take off again. **Thistlecrack** is another who could go over fences but there's undoubtedly more to come from him as a staying hurdler first. He proved well suited by the step up in trip when landing the Sefton Novices' Hurdle at Aintree and was perhaps unlucky not to bag another Grade 1 contest when beaten half a length at Punchestown after that. With doubts of various kinds about many at shorter odds in a wide-open market, the 25/1 on offer about the Colin Tizzard-trained Thistlecrack looks worth risking.

SELECTION Thistlecrack (25/1)

Cheltenham Gold Cup

It's **Vautour** who heads the betting again here at 4/1 or 5/1, but if we're taking him on in the King George on the grounds of unproven stamina (he's also offered at single-figure odds in the Champion Chase market!), then by the same logic he's even more opposable in the Gold Cup. **Coneygree** makes a lot more appeal back here than he does at Kempton, though he faces a potentially formidable Irish challenge to his Gold Cup crown if the likes of **Don Cossack**, **Don Poli** and **Djakadam** join Vautour in the line-up. The waters are muddied by the fact that Djakadam and Vautour share the same owner as well as trainer (Rich Ricci/Willie Mullins), while RSA Chase winner Don Poli is a stable-companion of that pair, as well as also being one of several in the Gigginstown camp along with last year's third **Road To Riches** and the again much-respected Don Cossack, not to mention **Valseur Lido** (also with Mullins) who won the Grade 1 novice at Punchestown in which Don Poli flopped. Doubtless the picture will become clearer by March, but at this stage, given his price (14/1 in places), it's last year's runner-up Djakadam who makes most appeal. That was a tremendous effort for a six-year-old, and a more mature Djakadam would have prospects of giving his trainer a belated first Gold Cup after becoming Willie Mullins' fifth runner-up last March. As if Gigginstown don't have a strong enough hand as it is, a more speculative each-way selection (available at 50/1) in those colours is the Noel Meade-trained **Wounded Warrior**. Third to Don Poli in the RSA and then runner-up to Valseur Lido at Punchestown, he's a sound jumper who is unexposed as a stayer and is another young chaser who could enter the Gold Cup picture over the winter.

SELECTIONS Djakadam (14/1)

Grand National

Shutthefrontdoor was the nearest thing to a success to emerge from this piece last year which selected him at 25/1 for Aintree before he was backed down to 6/1 favourite on the day, thanks, as anticipated, to the 'McCoy factor'. The fairy tale result didn't happen for the champion on his final ride in the race, but Shutthefrontdoor showed up very well for a long way until fading to finish a tired fifth behind **Many Clouds**. Shutthefrontdoor is one for the shortlist again, while Many Clouds is trading as the 20/1 favourite to become the first back-to-back winner since Red Rum in the 'seventies. History might appear to be against him, but Many Clouds is no ordinary National winner, posting the highest Timeform rating of any winner since Red Rum, in fact. That guarantees him a big burden again in 2016, though if **Silviniaco Conti** (among those close behind in the betting) is in the line-up, he might not find himself heading the weights. Last season's runner-up **Saint Are** is another prominent in the betting, but perhaps the most interesting runner from the 2015 renewal is **The Druids Nephew** (10/1 then, available at 25/1 for next year's race) who looked set to play a big part in the finish until falling five out when still going strongly in the lead. He won't be as well treated in next year's race, but he's still only eight and may have further improvement to make.

Gallant Oscar was a good third to The Druids Nephew in a competitive staying handicap at Cheltenham and followed that with an impressive win in a similar event at the Punchestown Festival. With few miles on the clock over fences for Tony Martin, it's not hard to see Gallant Oscar (available at 40/1) strengthening J. P. McManus's hand at Aintree next spring, while in the same colours **On The Fringe**, who has little left to prove in hunter chases, deserves a crack at a bigger prize and gave a fine display of jumping over the National fences when winning the Fox Hunters' in April. The sound-jumping **Paint The Clouds** (third to On The Fringe at Cheltenham) is a more speculative punt from the hunter chase ranks, but would be particularly interesting if maintaining his successful association with Sam Waley-Cohen who has such a good record around the National course. Paint The Clouds has form in top handicap company too, and was a well-backed fourth in the bet365 Gold Cup at Sandown in April when finishing a place behind **Le Reve** who is our other each-way selection at 40/1. Much improved in his second season over fences when he won two other handicaps at Sandown for Lucy Wadham,

Le Reve jumps well nowadays and, just a seven-year-old, hasn't had too many opportunities to show what he can do over long distances.

SELECTIONS **The Druids Nephew (25/1), Gallant Oscar and Le Reve (both 40/1 each-way)**

HAVE THE LAST WORD

Jumps winners last year included:
Many Clouds Won 25/1,
Wayward Prince Won 25/1 &
Caid du Berlais Won 10/1

Patience pays. Seize the value! Get the final verdict from David Cleary online. Every Saturday at 11:30
Login at timeform.com & on the App

     TIMEFORM

HORSES TO FOLLOW
WHAT'S THE POINT?

The Brightwells Festival (March) and April Sales at Cheltenham are two of the best sales to buy a horse which has made a bright start to its career in points, and in recent years the likes of Alisier d'Irlande, Tell Us More and Champers On Ice have changed hands there. Business at the two events was again buoyant earlier in the year, so let's take a look at the key lots which could make their mark under Rules for new connections in the coming months...

The sales-topper at the April Sale was **Born Survivor** who sold for £220,000 to prominent owners Richard and Lizzie Kelvin-Hughes, who'd bought Different Gravey (who's since won three of his four starts over hurdles) for £140,000 at the same sale in 2014. Born Survivor had made a successful point debut at Broughsane in Ireland just a week before when ridden by Jamie Codd and trained by his brother Willie Codd, who'd also consigned Alisier d'Irlande when he'd sold for £300,000. A full brother to Theatre Flame, who won over hurdles in June, Born Survivor has joined rising star trainer Dan Skelton, as has **North Hill Harvey** who was also purchased (for £100,000) by the Kelvin-Hughes' after making his own winning point debut at Chaddesley Corbett. Skelton himself signed for **Minella Experience** (£52,000) who was second (to the Gigginstown House Stud-owned Polymath) at Horse And Jockey on his Irish point debut.

Tell Us More's trainer Willie Mullins—along with his right-hand man Harold Kirk—bought four lots across the latest Festival and April Sales, with the most expensive being **Inspired Poet** at £155,000. This Yeats half-brother to the highly promising Minella Rocco (from the Juddmonte family which also contains Brian Boru and Cinders And Ashes) represented the same connections as Faugheen in Irish points and, having finished third in the aforementioned race won by Polymath on his debut, won his second start by eight lengths; he could be very interesting this season. £140,000-buy **Lucky Pass** made a winning point debut at Loughanmore by fourteen lengths, while £125,000-purchase **Sutton Manor** was runner-up on his sole outing in Irish points. Mullins' also bought the mare **Monbeg Rose** (£60,000) who'd won the first of her two starts between the flags. She has had a run for her new yard, finishing well beaten in a Tipperary bumper in May, but she pulled hard that day (when sent off at evens) and is worth another chance.

Anthony Bromley and David Minton's Highflyer Bloodstock were predictably busy at the Festival and April Sales too. Their most expensive outlay was the £120,000 paid for **Minella Awards**, who was a neck second on his sole start in Irish points;

the winner of that race at Tallow was **Crazyheart** (Polymath finished a distant third when making his debut) who was bought by trainer Paul Nolan for £110,000 at the Festival Sale. **Monbeg Charmer** and **Monbeg Legend** were both bought for £120,000, with the former an easy winner from two other finishers on his point debut and the latter a three-length winner of what appeared a more competitive Irish point on his own debut. Two other outright buys for Highflyer were **Semper Invicta**, who'd finished a close second to the odds-on Dounikos (trained by Gordon Elliott for Gigginstown) at Punchestown on his point debut, and **Fionn Mac Cul**, who'd finished third on both his point outings, including in the Broughsane race won by Born Survivor. The runner-up in the latter event was **Some Are Lucky**, who had finished third to the Elliott-trained subsequent Punchestown bumper winner Petit Mouchoir on his debut, and he was purchased at the April Sale by Tom George for £80,000. Highflyer also bought **Jessber's Dream** (£55,000), a six-length debut winner of a mares' point at Ballyvodock, and **Secret Door** (£45,000), who finished second to the Gigginstown-owned Shattered Love on his sole point outing.

Highflyer shared the purchases of a number of horses, including **Stowaway Magic** (with Nicky Henderson for £100,000) who won at Duhallow on his sole point start, **Icing On The Cake** (with Oliver Sherwood for £88,000) who fell when favourite for his point debut and then won at Inch, and the mare **Mia's Storm** (with Alan King for £40,000), a six-length winner on her debut at Loughanmore. Henderson will also train impressive all-the-way Inch winner **Unravelthemystery** (£80,000), the Ballynoe runner-up **Whatswrongwithyou** (£44,000), who's from the family of smart chaser Noble Alan, and the German-bred **Neumond** (£42,000), who was market leader when he fell on his point debut in the race won by Stowaway Magic. Sherwood will also train **Sporting Milan** (£50,000), a full brother to useful hurdler/chase winner Themilanhorse, and **The Fresh Prince** (£35,000).

Evan Williams signed for **De Bene Esse** (£75,000), who ran out in the Louth point won by Yorkhill last December and then won at Bandon by eight lengths, and **Positively Dylan** (£30,000), who was runner-up to Inspired Poet on his only run in the pointing field. Also on the buyers list was bloodstock agent Tom Malone who in the past has purchased the likes of Dodging Bullets, Mr Mole and Irving for Paul Nicholls. Malone broke the six-figure barrier twice at the April Sale, paying £200,000 for **Minella Aris** (who's from the family of Grade 1 bumper/hurdles winner Liss A Paoraigh) and £150,000 for **Red Hanrahan** (who's out of a half-sister to the very smart chaser Vic Venturi); both geldings fell on their Irish point debuts before winning their next outings.

WHAT'S THE POINT?

Minella Daddy is a half-brother to smart hurdler Noble Endeavor and, having finished runner-up on his second and third starts in Irish points, was sold to Peter Bowen for £60,000. **Inchiquin All Star** won the final one of his five outings in similar races and was purchased by Tim Vaughan for £50,000; he's out of a half-sister to the Irish staying chasers Empire of Dirt and Panther Claw. Donald McCain signed for **Battle of Shiloh** (won both his starts in Irish points) at £60,000 and **Golden Investment** (landed his sole outing in Irish points) at £42,000, as well as **Barney Dwan** (out of a half-sister to smart hurdler/chaser Geos and the French sire Kapgarde) and **Pride of Lecale** who were both picked up for £30,000. Eight-length Kildorrey winner **Corri Lindo** went to Tony Martin for £50,000, while Philip Hobbs now trains Kirkistown runner-up **Rolling Dylan** after paying £38,000 for him. Charlie Longsdon went to £35,000 to secure the mare **En Passe**, who's from the family of high-class chaser Benefficient, and to £30,000 to take home **Song of The Night**, who finished second to Monbeg Charmer at Kilmallock. Others to look out for this term are **Our Reward** (from the family of high-class chaser Snoopy Loopy) who was bought by Jamie Snowden for £30,000, **You Say What** who went to Neil King for £21,000 and **Sweetlittlekitty** (£25,000) and **Kit Casey** (£16,000) who have both joined Rebecca Curtis.

Three Key Lots:

Born Survivor (£220,000) joined Dan Skelton

Inspired Poet (£155,000) joined Willie Mullins

Stowaway Magic (£100,000) joined Nicky Henderson

REVIEW OF 2014/15

SECTION 4

TIMEFORM'S VIEW ON THE BIG RACES	82
TIMEFORM'S BEST OF 2014/15	107
2014/15 STATISTICS	114

HORSES TO FOLLOW

TIMEFORM'S VIEW

Chosen from the Timeform Formbook, here is Timeform's detailed analysis—compiled by our team of race reporters and supplemented by observations from Timeform's handicappers—of a selection of key races from the Cheltenham, Aintree and Punchestown festivals last spring.

CHELTENHAM Tuesday, March 10
GOOD (Old Course)

Sky Bet Supreme Novices' Hurdle (Grade 1) (1) 2m 110y

Pos	Btn	Horse	Age	Wgt	Eq	Trainer	Jockey	SP
1		DOUVAN (FR)	5	11-07		W. P. Mullins, Ireland	R. Walsh	2/1f
2	4½	SHANESHILL (IRE)	6	11-07		W. P. Mullins, Ireland	P. Townend	9/1
3	2½	SIZING JOHN	5	11-07		Henry de Bromhead, Ireland	J. J. Burke	25/1
4	3¼	L'AMI SERGE (IRE)	5	11-07		Nicky Henderson	Barry Geraghty	7/2
5	8	QEWY (IRE)	5	11-07		John Ferguson	Noel Fehily	14/1
6	3¼	TELL US MORE (IRE)	6	11-07		W. P. Mullins, Ireland	Bryan J. Cooper	12/1
7	3	ALVISIO VILLE (FR)	5	11-07		W. P. Mullins, Ireland	D. J. Casey	20/1
8	3¾	JOLLYALLAN	6	11-07		Harry Fry	A. P. McCoy	9/1
9	½	BENTELIMAR (IRE)	6	11-07		J. R. Barry, Ireland	Brian O'Connell	25/1
10	6	SOME PLAN (IRE)	7	11-07		Tom George	Paddy Brennan	25/1
11	4½	VELVET MAKER (FR)	6	11-07	(h)	A. J. Martin, Ireland	A. P. Heskin	40/1
ur		SEEDLING	6	11-07		Warren Greatrex	Gavin Sheehan	16/1

12 ran Race time: 3m 47.50 Closing sectional (3.85f): 55.9s (95.0%) Winning Owner: Mrs S. Ricci

There was a relatively small field for the top 2m novice hurdle of the season, and a few were clearly making up the numbers, but there's every reason to think this a good renewal among the principals, the winner chased home by last season's top bumper performer and a progressive Grade 1 winner, he himself turning abundant promise into a high-level of form in most taking fashion, everything about his effort suggesting he's a major contender for top hurdling honours in the next few seasons; interpretation of the time of the race supports taking a high view of the form, though the race was run in contrasting fashion to the Champion Hurdle, the overall pace much better in this; the times on the afternoon suggested the ground was a fair bit quicker on the hurdles course than the chase course, though the times for both fall within the range of good ground. **Douvan** well backed, on less testing ground than previously, added substance to the style of his previous hurdles wins with a most impressive success, his effort exceeding even those by the same connections' Champagne Fever and Vautour in the previous 2 runnings, one of the very best performances in this race; waited with, travelled well, good progress 2 out, led before last, jumped that really well to go further clear, kept on well run-in; he is clearly a top-class 2m hurdler in the making and will give his stable companion Faugheen something to think about this time in 2016 if all goes well, that a mouth-watering prospect, enough options in the meantime presumably to keep them apart. **Shaneshill** showed much improved form, runner-up at the Festival for the second year running, seeming well served by the drop back to 2m; handy, pushed along after 3 out, every chance before last, kept on well, no impression on winner; this was just his third start over hurdles and he's open to further improvement, and while he isn't the biggest, it may well be that he'll be switched to fences next season, given his stable's wealth of 2m hurdlers. **Sizing John** improved plenty, continuing an excellent first season over hurdles, and he's very much the type to carry on the progress as a chaser next time around; prominent, led 3 out, headed before last, one paced; may do better still, particularly as he's yet to be tried beyond 2m. **L'Ami Serge** held good form claims but wasn't able to show to best advantage, twice meeting trouble in running having also failed to travel well away from the mud, still likely to have been in contention for second without that; held up, not always fluent, hampered fourth, effort when hampered before 2 out, mistake there, one paced after; hopefully, he will get the chance to gain compensation, with the Top Novices' at Aintree an obvious option. **Qewy** ran respectably, just finding this much more demanding company too much for him; held up, effort 3 out, kept on straight, made little impression; he's the type that could make an impact in good handicaps, the run of that type of race likely to play to his strengths. **Tell Us More** on less testing ground than previously and back down in trip, didn't look at all out of place for much of the way, just faltering when it mattered; handy, every chance 2 out, weakened straight; overall, he's made a very promising start and remains with significant potential. **Alvisio Ville** was asked a stern question, given he'd come up short in terms of expectations at Leopardstown last time, and he lacked the maturity to make an impact, very much a work in progress and the type to really come into his own over fences next season, spared a hard race once his chance was gone; held up, shaken up after 3 out, made little impression, not unduly punished; will benefit from return to 2¼m+. **Jollyallan** had shown enough to think he could be competitive at this level and disappointed, his jumping not a problem particularly but his response to pressure underwhelming, later said to have lost a shoe and suffered exhaustion; held up, effort after 3 out, found little; in terms of physique, he'd be the most obvious of these to make a better chaser than a hurdler and he may well mature between now and the autumn, so he may yet fulfil his abundant potential.

Racing Post Arkle Challenge Trophy Chase (Grade 1) (1) 2m

Pos	Btn	Horse	Age	Wgt	Eq	Trainer	Jockey	SP
1		UN DE SCEAUX (FR)	7	11-04		W. P. Mullins, Ireland	R. Walsh	4/6f
2	6	GOD'S OWN (IRE)	7	11-04		Tom George	Paddy Brennan	33/1
3	2	JOSSES HILL (IRE)	7	11-04		Nicky Henderson	Barry Geraghty	12/1
4	5	VIBRATO VALTAT (FR)	6	11-04	(t)	Paul Nicholls	Sam Twiston-Davies	7/1
5	6	COURT MINSTREL (IRE)	8	11-04		Evan Williams	Paul Moloney	20/1
6	4½	SGT RECKLESS	8	11-04		Mick Channon	Brian Hughes	20/1
7	6	SMASHING (FR)	6	11-04		Henry de Bromhead, Ireland	J. J. Burke	20/1
8	2	CLARCAM (FR)	5	11-04	(t)	Gordon Elliott, Ireland	Bryan J. Cooper	16/1
9	10	THREE KINGDOMS (IRE)	6	11-04		John Ferguson	A. P. McCoy	14/1
pu		DUNRAVEN STORM (IRE)	10	11-04		Philip Hobbs	Richard Johnson	40/1
pu		SAIL BY THE SEA (IRE)	7	11-04	(t)	David Pipe	Tom Scudamore	33/1

11 ran   Race time: 3m 51.40   Closing sectional (3.55f): 54.5s (94.2%)   Winning Owner: E. O'Connell

Un de Sceaux set such a high standard that this can hardly be said to have been a competitive Arkle but it was certainly a good-quality one with plenty of depth to the form even behind the impressive winner, God's Own and Vibrato Valtat both having Grade 1 novice wins to their name already and hitting the frame along with one of last year's top novice hurdlers, Josses Hill; the winner set a strong pace, making the race a thorough test of jumping as well as stamina at the trip, and he did very well to maintain it whilst those that raced closest to him early all finished tired. **Un de Sceaux** handled the big occasion fine, helped perhaps by being brought into the parade ring late, typically sweating by post time but not boiling over as had been something of a pre-race concern, and he duly went on to confirm himself easily the best 2m novice chaser around, this performance bettered in recent runnings of the Arkle only by Sprinter Sacre and even then value for more than the winning margin, most impressive how he could set a strong gallop, really pour it on from a long way out and yet still be stronger than anything else at the finish; made most, jumped fluently and tanked along, shaken up soon after 2 out, asserted run-in, kept going well; he remains unbeaten on completed starts and is a genuinely outstanding prospect, not hard to envisage him as a Champion Chase winner of the future, entirely possible in fact that he'll take a lot of beating in that race this time next year, Sprinter Sacre and Sire de Grugy both having had their problems and set to be in the veteran stage by then, whilst Un de Sceaux could easily be improving still—there's no doubt whatsoever that there are still better performances in the locker. **God's Own** had some very smart form and plenty of experience, a Grade 1 novice winner at Punchestown last May who'd also defeated some big names at Exeter in the autumn, and after 11 weeks off (goes well fresh) he bounced back to his best, no match for Un de Sceaux but worth credit for being the only one to even briefly threaten that rival; held up, travelled smoothly, good progress ninth, chased leader after next, jumped right last 2, kept on; this track obviously wasn't a problem and he's capable of winning more good races in the future, still with the option of going back up in trip too, already a winner over 21f much earlier in career yet tried at that sort of distance only once since switched to fences. **Josses Hill** hasn't had the most convincing novice chase season it has to be said and there's still plenty of room for improvement in his jumping, but to run to the smart level he did here despite again not getting it quite right on that score is testament to the ability he has, and in fairness he was only careful at times as opposed to ever looking like falling; mid-division, jumped tentatively on occasions (notably the fifth and eighth), headway under pressure after 4 out, kept on well; it's possible it'll click with him in this sphere as he gains more experience and, if it does, he will better this form, well worth trying him back around 2½m at some stage. **Vibrato Valtat** shaped better than the distance beaten suggests and can be viewed as still in good form, probably paying the price to some extent for getting close to Un de Sceaux earlier than either God's Own or Josses Hill; mid-division, travelled well, went handy before fifth, chased leader 4 out, pushed along after next, no extra run-in; he's had an excellent novice season over fences and should give a good account at Aintree and/or Punchestown.

Stan James Champion Hurdle Challenge Trophy (Grade 1) (1) 2m 110y

Pos	Btn	Horse	Age	Wgt	Eq	Trainer	Jockey	SP
1		FAUGHEEN (IRE)	7	11-10		W. P. Mullins, Ireland	R. Walsh	4/5f
2	1½	ARCTIC FIRE (GER)	6	11-10	(h)	W. P. Mullins, Ireland	Daniel Mullins	20/1
3	5	HURRICANE FLY (IRE)	11	11-10		W. P. Mullins, Ireland	P. Townend	8/1
4	1¾	JEZKI (IRE)	7	11-10	(h)	Mrs J. Harrington, Ireland	A. P. McCoy	6/1
5	½	THE NEW ONE (IRE)	7	11-10		Nigel Twiston-Davies	Sam Twiston-Davies	10/3
6	1	KITTEN ROCK (FR)	5	11-10		E. J. O'Grady, Ireland	Noel Fehily	28/1
7	6	BERTIMONT (FR)	5	11-10	(t)	Dan Skelton	Harry Skelton	100/1
8	12	VANITEUX (FR)	6	11-10		Nicky Henderson	Barry Geraghty	25/1

8 ran Race time: 3m 50.90 Closing sectional (3.85f): 54.3s (99.2%) Winning Owner: Mrs S. Ricci

TIMEFORM'S VIEW

A relatively small field but a representative one, with 2 previous winners in the line up, as well as the last 2 winners of the Baring Bingham, the form of nearly all the significant trials well represented too, Faugheen boasting the best form this season with his win at Kempton; as such there was a predictable air to the outcome, though that doesn't tell the whole story, Faugheen benefiting from a really well-judged ride in front, the pace picking up only 3 out, the runner-up perhaps a shade better than the distances indicate; Faugheen led home a clean sweep on a remarkable day for his stable, Willie Mullins winning this race for the third time in 5 years as well as landing a third successive Supreme and the inaugural Grade 1 running of the Mares Hurdle, with the Arkle thrown in for good measure. **Faugheen** had shown the best form in this division this season when winning the Christmas Hurdle at Kempton last time and hardly needed to improve to follow up, taking his winning run over hurdles to 8, given a well-judged waiting-in-front ride from Ruby Walsh, fluffing the second-last the most anxious moment for his supporters; led, travelled well, quickened 3 out, not fluent next, ridden straight, found extra; he is open to improvement still and likely to add further successes before he has to meet Douvan, hopefully in this race in 2016. **Arctic Fire** proved better than ever, progressing fully 20 lb this season, since his second in last year's County Hurdle, if anything a shade better than the result, coming from off the pace in a steadily-run race; held up, headway 3 out, kept on well straight, chased leader run-in, kept on; given his stable's wealth of talent in this division, it wasn't entirely surprising that his trainer suggested a campaign geared to a challenge for the Melbourne Cup in November. **Hurricane Fly** ran a gallant race, strictly a bit below his season's best, but this not playing to his current strengths anything like so well as the races he contests in Ireland; in touch, travelled well, effort home turn, chased leader before last, not quicken run-in; he's been a tremendous horse in his time, for ability, attitude and durability a fantastic standard-setter for the sport, and if this proves to be his last appearance at Cheltenham, he went out with honour, and there may yet be a swansong to come at Punchestown. **Jezki** failed to meet expectations, behind Hurricane Fly yet again and with no excuses this time, just not at the moment the horse he was in this race in 2014 (when he got the perfect ride from Barry Geraghty); prominent, challenged 2 out, one paced straight, held when mistake last; he followed up at Punchestown a year ago, but such a prospect looks less likely now, whether he faces Faugheen or Hurricane Fly. **The New One** failed to meet expectations, his lack of speed when faced with this sort of test finding him out, though the way he was hanging in the straight suggests all might not have been well; prominent, ridden before 2 out, not quicken, hung left straight; he will benefit from a return to further at this level and, if he remains over hurdles, then the World Hurdle would surely be the aim at this meeting in 2016.

CHELTENHAM Wednesday, March 11
GOOD (Old Course)

Neptune Investment Management Novices' Hurdle (Baring Bingham) (Grade 1) (1) 2m 5f

Pos	Btn	Horse	Age	Wgt	Eq	Trainer	Jockey	SP
1		WINDSOR PARK (IRE)	6	11-07		D. K. Weld, Ireland	Davy Russell	9/2
2	3¾	PARLOUR GAMES	7	11-07	(h)	John Ferguson	A. P. McCoy	13/2
3	1¼	NICHOLS CANYON	5	11-07		W. P. Mullins, Ireland	R. Walsh	7/2f

TIMEFORM'S VIEW

4	nk	VYTA DU ROC (FR)	6	11-07		Nicky Henderson	Barry Geraghty	15/2
5	nk	SNOW FALCON (IRE)	5	11-07		Noel Meade, Ireland	Paul Carberry	20/1
6	½	OUTLANDER (IRE)	7	11-07		W. P. Mullins, Ireland	Bryan J. Cooper	4/1
7	1½	ORDO AB CHAO (IRE)	6	11-07		Alan King	Wayne Hutchinson	10/1
8	38	WARRANTOR (IRE)	6	11-07	(t)	Warren Greatrex	Gavin Sheehan	33/1
9	nk	BEAST OF BURDEN (IRE)	6	11-07		Rebecca Curtis	P. Townend	8/1
10	33	ANTEROS (IRE)	7	11-07	(t)	Sophie Leech	Paul Moloney	100/1

10 ran   Race time: 5m 07.40   Winning Owner: Dr R. Lambe

With a roll of honour that includes Istabraq, Hardy Eustace, The New One and Faugheen, it's fair to say that this is a race with a rich history of producing top-class hurdlers and, although perhaps not quite such a strong renewal as some in recent times, this was a really competitive race in its own right and there looks to be plenty of substance to the result with winners of the Challow and Deloitte respectively filling the places; the bare form can be put under some scrutiny, however, as it wasn't a truly-run race and they finished well bunched, perhaps no coincidence that a trio with at least useful Flat form came to the fore—Vyta du Roc should be rated second though, as he was the main threat to the winner before a last-flight blunder. **Windsor Park** had been held back to some extent by his jumping when fourth to Outlander and second to Nichols Canyon on his previous couple of starts but he's entitled to still be learning in that regard and this time put everything together to turn form around with the Willie Mullins pair, helped by a return to positive tactics, well positioned throughout and equipped to cope with the relative test of speed (useful winner on the Flat), though that's not to take anything away from him; led until fourth, remained prominent and jumped/travelled well, went on again 2 out, looked in control (yet to be asked for maximum effort) when left clear by Vyta du Roc's blunder at the last and was just kept up to work; he won 2 from 2 on the Flat last year and could reportedly return to that sphere at some point this year, a possible for the Ascot Gold Cup, but as a hurdler he's likely to progress further too. **Parlour Games** could have been asked to do little more than he has since the autumn, a Grade 1 winner when last seen 10 weeks ago and running another cracker in an even deeper race this time, the emphasis on speed again in his favour even though, like last time, he was patiently ridden; dropped out, travelled well, crept closer 3 out, chased leaders after next, left second last, kept on; he's fresh for the time of year and should give a good account if taking his chance at Aintree/Punchestown. **Nichols Canyon** had no problem with the 3f longer trip, unsurprisingly so given his staying Flat form, and backed up all of the improvement he'd shown to win the Deloitte last time despite Windsor Park turning the tables on him; tracked pace, took keen hold, close up 3 out, not fluent 2 out, ridden when left in a place last, one paced; he does have a high knee action and has always gone particularly well in the mud, so perhaps back on more testing ground he will improve again. **Vyta du Roc** has had an excellent season going right back to last summer, worth credit for the consistency he's shown, yet to disappoint, progressing with each start in fact, and he'd definitely have finished second and may even have given the winner plenty to think about—mindful how well he responds to pressure—but for making a complete mess of the final flight; chased leaders, disputed lead 2 out, ridden when chance-ending mistake last, lost all momentum but still rallied up the hill to almost snatch a place; as mentioned last time, he will stay

TIMEFORM'S VIEW | 87

further than 21f, whilst thinking longer term he has the size for chasing. **Snow Falcon** had a lot to find but is young/lightly raced and seemed to excel himself up in grade, clearly a smart novice, perhaps suited by the less testing ground than he'd encountered previously over hurdles (bumper runs all came on good); waited with, headway 3 out, ridden after next, kept on. **Outlander** remains in good form and wasn't necessarily seen to best effect the way this developed, likely to have benefited from a stronger pace, although it's worth mentioning that when it came to the crunch he did look a little ungainly, as was the case in bumpers earlier in his career; raced wide, mid-field, took strong hold, mistake seventh, headway before next, held when hung left approaching last, one paced; there's no doubt that he's talented, perhaps more so than bare form up to now suggests, and he does have the physique, pedigree and pointing background to imply his future will be over fences.

RSA Chase (Grade 1) (1) 3m 110y

Pos	Btn	Horse	Age	Wgt	Eq	Trainer	Jockey	SP
1		DON POLI (IRE)	6	11-04		W. P. Mullins, Ireland	Bryan J. Cooper	13/8f
2	6	SOUTHFIELD THEATRE (IRE)	7	11-04		Paul Nicholls	Sam Twiston-Davies	13/2
3	1½	WOUNDED WARRIOR (IRE)	6	11-04		Noel Meade, Ireland	Paul Carberry	12/1
4	hd	ADRIANA DES MOTTES (FR)	5	10-09		W. P. Mullins, IRE	R. Walsh	14/1
5	½	IF IN DOUBT (IRE)	7	11-04		Philip Hobbs	A. P. McCoy	12/1
6	16	KINGS PALACE (IRE)	7	11-04	(t)	David Pipe	Tom Scudamore	4/1
7	29	THE YOUNG MASTER	6	11-04	(s)	Neil Mulholland	Barry Geraghty	11/2
pu		APACHE JACK (IRE)	7	11-04	(s)	Ms Sandra Hughes, Ireland	Davy Condon	33/1

8 ran   Race time: 6m 09.20 Closing sectional (3.55f): 55.2s (96.9%)   Winning Owner: Gigginstown House Stud

A good field for the season's leading staying novice chase, acknowledging the absence of Gold Cup-bound Coneygree, and the well-backed winner put up an effort well up to the recent standards for the race in powering away from some smart rivals on the run-in, providing Ireland with their sixth winner of the race in the last 7 years; The Young Master and King's Palace forced a sound gallop and there was a strong emphasis on both jumping and stamina, befitting a championship novice. **Don Poli** was all the rage in the betting back from 10 weeks off and maintained an unblemished record over fences, strictly speaking not having to improve much on form that already set the standard but again most impressive, notably with his strength at the finish of a soundly-run race, forging right away in the manner of one well up to competing in the top staying chases, easy to see him emulating his connections' Sir des Champs, who also won the Martin Pipe and a Grade 1 novice chase at this meeting before going on to make his presence felt in open company, no surprise to see Don Poli back here next year among the leading contenders for the Gold Cup; settled in mid-division, he went in snatches a little but jumped very well and was upsides back on the bridle 4 out, sent on soon after the next and storming clear up the hill, affirming that further than 3m will suit. **Southfield Theatre** has had a cracking first season over fences and ran as well as he ever has to finish second at this meeting for the second year running, unsurprisingly well suited by the return to 3m, seeing it out thoroughly; chased leaders, not fluent ninth, blundered 4 out, effort soon after next, stuck to task, no match for winner; he's sure to keep giving a good account and, given how well the stable does with similar types, may do better still. **Wounded Warrior** couldn't get any closer to Don Poli than he'd managed at Gowran earlier in the season but ran a stormer in his own right back from 8 weeks off, again strong at the finish over this trip, sure to stay further if required; held up, jumped soundly, headway under pressure after 3 out, chased leaders straight, kept on well, took third dying strides. **Adriana des Mottes** looked to have plenty on even in receipt of a sex allowance and excelled herself with a very useful effort, the longer trip presumably the catalyst, no reason to doubt it judged on how she moved; held up, travelled as well as any, not fluent twelfth, fourteenth, headway 3 out, met some trouble briefly home turn, chased leaders straight, one paced. **If In Doubt** taking in this race instead of another handicap, ran well on form despite doing a fair bit wrong, a sign of his ability that he had running left in the finish after a series of mistakes, even better to come should he iron those out; dropped out, mistakes ninth, tenth, shaken up fourteenth, headway when not fluent again 3 out, stayed on, never nearer; it's possible he'll never be a consistently good jumper, but there's no doubt he's got more ability than he's revealed so far over fences and, as such, he'd have to be a most interesting runner in such as the Hennessy next autumn. **Kings Palace** is obviously better than this but mirrored 2013/14 in losing an unbeaten record for the season in a Grade 1 at this meeting, as then probably doing a bit too much in front, though a blunder—not dissimilar to the one he made at Newbury last time—clearly didn't help; disputed lead until fifth, remained prominent, mistake eighth, went on after tenth, bad mistake 4 out, ridden when headed before 2 out, weakened.

Betway Queen Mother Champion Chase (Grade 1) (1) 2m

Pos	Btn	Horse	Age	Wgt	Eq	Trainer	Jockey	SP
1		DODGING BULLETS	7	11-10	(t)	Paul Nicholls	Sam Twiston-Davies	9/2
2	1¼	SOMERSBY (IRE)	11	11-10	(s)	Mick Channon	Brian Hughes	33/1
3	1¾	SPECIAL TIARA	8	11-10		Henry de Bromhead, Ireland	Noel Fehily	18/1
4	7	SIRE DE GRUGY (FR)	9	11-10		Gary Moore	Jamie Moore	5/2
5	7	SIMPLY NED (IRE)	8	11-10		Nicky Richards	Brian Harding	14/1
6	4½	SAVELLO (IRE)	9	11-10	(h)	A. J. Martin, Ireland	Bryan J. Cooper	40/1
7	9	SIZING EUROPE (IRE)	13	11-10	(s)	Henry de Bromhead, Ireland	J. J. Burke	22/1
8	7	MR MOLE (IRE)	7	11-10	(t)	Paul Nicholls	A. P. McCoy	13/2
pu		SPRINTER SACRE (FR)	9	11-10		Nicky Henderson	Barry Geraghty	9/4f

9 ran   Race time: 3m 53.30   Winning Owner: Martin Broughton & Friends

A fascinating Champion Chase, full of imponderables, the outstanding 2013 winner Sprinter Sacre back to try and regain the crown having had all sorts of problems over the last 18 months, whilst last year's winner Sire de Grugy had also missed much of this season through injury; it was those two former winners that headed the pre-race ratings but neither of them were even close to their best, whilst Champagne Fever was a late non-runner, so it was a much weaker renewal in the event than looked possible beforehand, a point that's highlighted best by the fact that the 11-y-o Somersby and Special Tiara, who'd never quite looked up to this level previously, weren't beaten far into second/third, and it certainly isn't a vintage Champion Chase in form terms; the result is one to be believed, however, as Special Tiara set a good pace that made it fair to all, tactics not the reason why nothing held up got seriously involved. **Dodging Bullets** has been a completely different horse since fitted with a tongue strap, winning the Tingle Creek, Clarence House and Champion Chase on the bounce, and although he isn't in quite the same league as some that have managed the same feat there's no doubt that he's been the best horse in the division—a below-par one this time around—over the course of the season so far, not needing to improve any more here, actually beating Somersby by less than he had at Sandown in December; he was prominent throughout but kept a few lengths off the leader until moving upsides after 3 out, still travelling strongly then and leading at the next where he wasn't totally fluent (jumped well otherwise), tackled from the last and battling well, his resolution certainly not questionable nowadays; with the exciting Arkle winner Un de Sceaux coming on the scene it's likely to be tougher for Dodging Bullets to win this again next year but he won't always come up against him and is young enough to potentially have a few years left in him at this level; he'll reportedly be given time off now ahead of next season. **Somersby** has been competing at the top level for several years now, this his seventh Cheltenham Festival, and it's the fourth time that he's been placed at the meeting, still able to show the high-class form necessary to be competitive in Grade 1s even at the age of 11, briefly looking the winner of this as he came through to press Dodging Bullets; mid-division, crept closer before seventh, not fluent 4 out, close up next, every chance from the last but had no more to give late on. **Special Tiara** was better than ever when accounting for Balder Succes at Kempton 11 weeks ago and produced another career best to be placed in an open Grade 1 for the first time, arguably worth some extra credit given he was responsible for the fairly strong pace, but he does seem ideally suited by aggressive tactics; forced pace and was clear by the fourth, reduced advantage seventh, joined after 3 out, headed next, kept on. **Sire de Grugy** had something of a rushed preparation, not back for the season until Newbury just over 4 weeks ago and then, after that hadn't gone to plan, given another run (on heavy ground) only 18 days ago, far from ideal coming back into a championship race, and he was some way below his best; held up, hit sixth, headway under pressure after 4 out, chased leaders before 2 out but failed to quicken; although it's easy to pick holes in his Chepstow form there was enough in that effort to suggest he at least retains most of his ability and, assuming he can stay injury free, there could well be more Grade 1s to be won with him, be it this season or next. **Sprinter Sacre** put up one of the truly outstanding performances of all time when he won this with stacks in hand 2 years ago but the well-documented problems that he's had since have clearly taken their toll and he was clearly amiss 8 weeks after a satisfactory return behind Dodging Bullets at Ascot; mid-division, jumped well and took keen hold, headway 4 out, shaken up after next but found nothing and was quickly pulled up.

Weatherbys Champion Bumper (Standard Open National Hunt Flat) (Grade 1) (1) 2m 110y

Pos	Btn	Horse	Age	Wgt	Eq	Trainer	Jockey	SP
1		MOON RACER (IRE)	6	11-05		David Pipe	Tom Scudamore	9/2f
2	1½	MODUS	5	11-05	(h)	Robert Stephens	Tom O'Brien	33/1
3	1½	WAIT FOR ME (FR)	5	11-05		Philip Hobbs	Richard Johnson	9/1
4	nk	YANWORTH	5	11-05		Alan King	A. P. McCoy	16/1
5	4	VIGIL (IRE)	6	11-05		D. K. Weld, Ireland	Pat Smullen	8/1
6	hd	SUPASUNDAE	5	11-05		Henry de Bromhead, Ireland	J. J. Burke	17/2
7	1¾	THEO'S CHARM (IRE)	5	11-05		Nick Gifford	Tom Cannon	100/1
8	1	MONTANA BELLE (IRE)	5	10-12	(t)	Stuart Crawford, Ireland	Mr Steven Crawford	50/1
9	4½	BAY OF FREEDOM (IRE)	6	11-05		Peter Fahey, Ireland	Noel Fehily	100/1
10	1¾	BELLSHILL (IRE)	5	11-05		W. P. Mullins, Ireland	R. Walsh	14/1
11	3	GENERAL PRINCIPLE (IRE)	6	11-05		Gordon Elliott, Ireland	Bryan J. Cooper	9/1
12	1	GHOST RIVER	5	11-05		Peter Bowen	Sean Bowen	40/1
13	½	AU QUART DE TOUR (FR)	5	11-05		W. P. Mullins, Ireland	Daniel Mullins	25/1
14	3	DAVY DOUBT (IRE)	6	11-05		Warren Greatrex	Gavin Sheehan	40/1

TIMEFORM'S VIEW

15	¾	LIVELOVELAUGH (IRE)	5	11-05		W. P. Mullins, Ireland	Ms K. Walsh	28/1
16	7	O O SEVEN (IRE)	5	11-05		Nicky Henderson	Barry Geraghty	40/1
17	3½	ALWAYS LION (IRE)	5	11-05		Ben Pauling	David Bass	100/1
18	½	UP FOR REVIEW (IRE)	6	11-05		W. P. Mullins, Ireland	D. J. Casey	40/1
19	3½	STONE HARD (IRE)	5	11-05		W. P. Mullins, Ireland	P. Townend	10/1
20	5	WESTERN WAY (IRE)	6	11-05	(b)	Don Cantillon	Denis O'Regan	66/1
21	13	JETSTREAM JACK (IRE)	5	11-05		Gordon Elliott, Ireland	Davy Condon	14/1
22	23	NEATLY PUT	5	11-05		Denis Hogan, Ireland	Denis Hogan	150/1
pu		BORDINI (FR)	5	11-05		W. P. Mullins, Ireland	Mr P. W. Mullins	7/1

23 ran   Race time: 3m 49.50 Closing sectional (3.85f): 54.4s (98.4%)   Winning Owner: Professor Caroline Tisdall & Bryan Drew

As ever for a Champion Bumper, this field featured plenty of cracking prospects for jumping, the winner chief among them, though the bare form may not quite match some of the top-class efforts seen in the race in recent seasons, this running notable for the Irish challenge falling short, each of the first 4 trained in Britain; the gallop was even rather than strong and the key tactical feature was arguably that 4 of the first 5 saved ground by racing up the inside until the home turn. **Moon Racer** was backed into favouritism 5 months on from winning over C&D in October and put up another smart effort to maintain an unbeaten record, different tactics forced on him due to a standing start but no bad thing as it turned out, actually getting a very smooth run up the inner, though stamping his seal on things in a manner that leaves little doubt he was the best horse in the race; slowly into stride, held up, travelled fluently, headway from 3f out, led over 1f out, stayed on strongly; a good-topped gelding with the physique for jumping, it'll be no surprise to see him back here next March as a leading contender for top novice hurdle honours. **Modus** in first-time hood, produced best effort to date as he stepped up on his eighth in this last season, a cracking effort considering he'd been off 11 months, also starting his run from an unpromising position, albeit getting a smooth passage up the inside; slowly into stride, raced well off the pace, took strong hold, good progress over 2f out, finished well; clearly has the ability to win good races over hurdles, though he's bred and built for the Flat, and could make into a useful performer at least if tried in that sphere. **Wait For Me** showed smart form less than a month on from his impressive winning debut, underscoring a highly promising start to his career, clearly a top prospect for jumping next season; mid-division, travelled well, headway 3f out, challenged over 1f out, kept on. **Yanworth** produced best effort to date back from 12 weeks off and maybe deserves a bit of extra credit, having the trickiest run through of the frame finishers; held up, travelled as well as any, headway 3f out, shuffled back home turn, rallied over 1f out, ran on; in good hands and should do well over jumps, even if not so imposing as some in the field. **Vigil** ran well after 10 weeks off, matching his finishing position in this in 2014, seemingly just not quite good enough; prominent, travelled well, challenged over 2f out, every chance approaching final 1f, no extra. **Supasundae** ran creditably on first outing for 12 weeks/since leaving Andrew Balding, albeit unable to uphold Ascot form with the runner-up, not quite so strong at the finish at this stiffer track, having gone from the front this time; soon led, went with zest, effort 2f out, headed approaching final 1f, no extra. **Theo's Charm** was a huge price and acquitted himself very well in this more competitive environment, again shaping like a stayer; mid-division, outpaced 3f out, rallied well over 1f out, finished with running left; he's got the raw materials of a really good long-term prospect. **Montana Belle** wasn't really seen to best effect after 4 months off and ran well in the circumstances, likely to have at least matched her form from last time granted a smoother run through; held up, headway out wide from 3f out, effort 2f out, ran on, never nearer; should do well in mares novice hurdles next season. **Bay of Freedom** ran well after 5 months off, even though never in the hunt, pretty encouraging in the circumstances, especially bearing in mind he's bred to stay a lot further than 2m; in rear, headway over 2f out, kept on, never landed a blow. **Bellshill** wasn't disgraced in faring the best of the Mullins contingent after 10 weeks off, though couldn't improve any more, a lot further behind Vigil than at Leopardstown just after Christmas; mid-division, pushed along 3f out, not quicken, made no impression. **General Principle** a chaser on looks, wasn't seen to best effect after going the circuitous route and remains a really good prospect for jumping, sure to stay further when his attentions are turned that way; held up, headway out wide over 3f out, chased leaders 2f out, weakened approaching final 1f.

CHELTENHAM Thursday, March 12
GOOD to FIRM (New Course)

JLT Novices' Chase (Golden Miller) (Grade 1) (1) 2m 4f

Pos	Btn	Horse	Age	Wgt	Eq	Trainer	Jockey	SP
1		VAUTOUR (FR)	6	11-04		W. P. Mullins, Ireland	R. Walsh	6/4f
2	15	APACHE STRONGHOLD (IRE)	7	11-04		Noel Meade, Ireland	Paul Carberry	7/1
3	sh	VALSEUR LIDO (FR)	6	11-04		W. P. Mullins, Ireland	Bryan J. Cooper	9/2
4	3	IRISH SAINT (FR)	6	11-04	(t)	Paul Nicholls	Noel Fehily	8/1
5	nk	PTIT ZIG (FR)	6	11-04		Paul Nicholls	Sam Twiston-Davies	11/2
6	25	TANGO DE JUILLEY (FR)	7	11-04		Venetia Williams	Aidan Coleman	40/1
7	8	SPLASH OF GINGE	7	11-04		Nigel Twiston-Davies	Ryan Hatch	14/1
8	8	COLOUR SQUADRON (IRE)	9	11-04	(b+t)	Philip Hobbs	A. P. McCoy	18/1

8 ran Race time: 4m 46.30 Closing sectional (3.84f): 53.9s (102.0%) Winning Owner: Mrs S. Ricci

Vautour produced the best performance in the short history of this race, beating some promising rivals who'd shown a smart level of form in comprehensive fashion, his jumping outstanding for a novice, his win giving his stable a clean sweep of the Grade 1 novice chases at the Festival, Vautour every bit as impressive as Un de Sceaux and Don Poli, the trio having the potential to return in 2016 and dominate again in the Grade 1 open races. **Vautour** had form over fences that didn't have much depth to it but he'd been a most taking winner of the Supreme Novices' over hurdles at this meeting in 2014 and returned for an even more impressive success over fences, showing a level of form good enough to have won the Ryanair later on the card (or the Champion Chase); made all, jumped superbly, travelled strongly, in command straight, stayed on strongly, impressive; clearly a top-class chaser who will make a major impact in the best races in 2015/6 if all goes well, every bit as promising as his successful stable companions in the Arkle and RSA earlier in the week. **Apache Stronghold** confirmed placings with the third from last time, running his best race yet, but he was completely outclassed by the winner; held up, travelled well, good progress 3 out, chased leader straight, no impression, kept on to regain second final 100 yds; he's a smart young chaser and may yet have more to offer, likely to continue to pay his way, given the Irish programme for such horses. **Valseur Lido** was closely matched with the runner-up from last time and ran up to best, this just his fourth start over fences, though he may need a step up in trip to find further improvement; handy, travelled well, effort after 3 out, second when rider dropped whip before last, no impression on winner; he may yet be capable of better and the Irish programme should ensure that he has a successful time next season. **Irish Saint** ran up to his best, if anything deserving extra credit after pestering the leader, particularly on the final circuit, those exertions not appearing to tell too much against him as he saw the race out thoroughly; pressed leader for much of way, hit 4 out, left behind next, kept on again run-in; he'd skipped Cheltenham for Aintree in the previous 2 seasons, but clearly the track was no problem for him. **Ptit Zig** ran respectably and, though he made a couple of mistakes in the latter stages there were no obvious excuses, perhaps just not quite so promising as his wins in lesser races indicate; handy, yet to be asked for effort when mistake 4 out, pushed along after, not quicken straight, mistake 2 out, kept on.

Ryanair Chase (Festival) (Grade 1) (1) 2m 5f

Pos	Btn	Horse	Age	Wgt	Eq	Trainer	Jockey	SP
1		UXIZANDRE (FR)	7	11-10	(v)	Alan King	A. P. McCoy	16/1
2	5	MA FILLEULE (FR)	7	11-03		Nicky Henderson	Barry Geraghty	5/1
3	3¼	DON COSSACK (GER)	8	11-10	(t)	Gordon Elliott, IRE	Bryan J. Cooper	5/2f
4	2¾	EDUARD (IRE)	7	11-10		Nicky Richards	Brian Harding	16/1
5	4	JOHNS SPIRIT (IRE)	8	11-10		Jonjo O'Neill	Richie McLernon	8/1
6	10	HIDDEN CYCLONE (IRE)	10	11-10	(s)	John Joseph Hanlon, Ireland	Andrew J. McNamara	12/1
7	1¾	BALDER SUCCES (FR)	7	11-10		Alan King	Wayne Hutchinson	7/1
8	8	WONDERFUL CHARM (FR)	7	11-10	(s+t)	Paul Nicholls	Sam Twiston-Davies	16/1
9	2¾	TAQUIN DU SEUIL (FR)	8	11-10		Jonjo O'Neill	Noel Fehily	14/1
10	sh	THIRD INTENTION (IRE)	8	11-10	(t)	Colin Tizzard	Daryl Jacob	66/1
11	12	DOUBLE ROSS (IRE)	9	11-10	(t)	Nigel Twiston-Davies	Ryan Hatch	66/1
12	9	FOXROCK (IRE)	7	11-10		T. M. Walsh, Ireland	A. P. Heskin	12/1
pu		WISHFULL THINKING	12	11-10	(t)	Philip Hobbs	Richard Johnson	28/1
pu		BALLYCASEY (IRE)	8	11-10		W. P. Mullins, Ireland	R. Walsh	22/1

14 ran Race time: 5m 01.20 Winning Owner: Mr John P. McManus

An up-to-standard renewal of this Grade 1, despite a notable list of intended runners that had fallen by the wayside in recent weeks—Cue Card, Al Ferof and last year's winner Dynaste among them; not all of those with best form gave their running, and the winner sprang a surprise, though his win here in the autumn promised much and he finally delivered on that, well worth crediting with the apparent improvement shown. **Uxizandre** in change of headgear, bounced back to form in remarkable fashion, much improved and again showing how well he handles this track; led, jumped very well, travelled strongly, pressed on again home turn, kept on well run-in, unchallenged; his options are limited for the rest of the season, given his trainer's preference for sticking left handed, with the Melling Chase at Aintree the obvious one, a win in the Manifesto as a novice suggesting he'll go well again there. **Ma Filleule** ran up to her best in finishing second at this meeting for the second year running, needing no excuses against a much-improved rival; in touch, travelled well, chased leader 3 out, no extra final 50 yds; worth another try around 3m and the Bowl at Aintree looks a good option. **Don Cossack** strong in the betting, shaped well in defeat and, under different circumstances, would have given the winner something to think about, underlining he's a totally different horse this season; prominent and travelled well but lost ground when pecking at the twelfth and only just getting going when badly hampered approaching the second last (lost all momentum), hitting that for good measure yet still finishing with running left as he claimed a place after the last; will remain of plenty of interest. **Eduard** after 3 months off, ran up to best, consistent in defeat in a light campaign; prominent, travelled well, second 3 out, not quicken straight, third when mistake last. **Johns Spirit** ran creditably, though this second crack at Grade 1 company highlighted limitations, no excuses on a track that he handles so well; held up, travelled well, steady headway ninth, mistake 4 out, not quicken before last and faltered late on; probably not the easiest to place, though the Silver Trophy at the next meeting here may be an option. **Hidden Cyclone** had finished second in last year's Ryanair and was unable to match that, this race stronger form, though his jumping left something to be desired as well; chased leader, travelled well, mistake second, clouted sixth, ridden after 3 out, no extra after 2 out and beaten when mistake last.

Ladbrokes World Hurdle (Grade 1) (1) 3m

Pos	Btn	Horse	Age	Wgt	Eq	Trainer	Jockey	SP
1		COLE HARDEN (IRE)	6	11-10	(t)	Warren Greatrex	Gavin Sheehan	14/1
2	3¼	SAPHIR DU RHEU (FR)	6	11-10		Paul Nicholls	Sam Twiston-Davies	5/1f
3	3¼	ZARKANDAR (IRE)	8	11-10	(b+t)	Paul Nicholls	Noel Fehily	6/1
4	nk	AT FISHERS CROSS (IRE)	8	11-10	(b)	Rebecca Curtis	A. P. McCoy	14/1
5	3¾	WHISPER (FR)	7	11-10		Nicky Henderson	Barry Geraghty	8/1
6	½	UN TEMPS POUR TOUT (IRE)	6	11-10	(t)	David Pipe	Tom Scudamore	9/1
7	1¼	SEEYOUATMIDNIGHT	7	11-10		Sandy Thomson	Brian Hughes	16/1
8	5	ZAIDPOUR (FR)	9	11-10	(s)	W. P. Mullins, Ireland	P. Townend	66/1
9	2½	JETSON (IRE)	10	11-10		Mrs J. Harrington, Ireland	Davy Russell	14/1
10	9	LIEUTENANT COLONEL	6	11-10	(s)	Ms Sandra Hughes, Ireland	Bryan J. Cooper	7/1
11	¾	REVE DE SIVOLA (FR)	10	11-10		Nick Williams	Daryl Jacob	20/1
12	2½	BLUE FASHION (IRE)	6	11-10		Nicky Henderson	David Bass	20/1
13	7	TIGER ROLL (IRE)	5	11-10	(t)	Gordon Elliott, Ireland	Davy Condon	50/1
14	6	MONKSLAND (IRE)	8	11-10		Noel Meade, Ireland	Paul Carberry	14/1
15	2¼	AUBUSSON (FR)	6	11-10		Nick Williams	Lizzie Kelly	50/1
16	9	ABBYSSIAL (IRE)	5	11-10		W. P. Mullins, Ireland	R. Walsh	14/1

16 ran   Race time: 5m 41.00   Winning Owner: Mrs Jill Eynon & Mr Robin Eynon

There were shades of the 2006 renewal, won by May Way de Solzen, in this year's World Hurdle, the winner from 12 months ago, More of That, currently on the sidelines just as Inglis Drever was then, whilst last year's runner-up Annie Power had gone for the mares race earlier in the week, leaving a wide open, competitive race but one that lacked real star quality, and Cole Harden's performance is rated lower than any other recent winner; Cole Harden made all of the running but did so at a good tempo, underlined by a time that was quicker than the earlier Pertemps Final. **Cole Harden** arrived with something to prove after a disappointing run in the Cleeve but had been operated on for a breathing problem since and not only got back on track but resumed his progress from earlier in the season to land the staying division's premier event, not achieving so much as most winners of this race but full value for it on the day, setting a good gallop and proving willing/determined; made all, hit seventh (generally jumped much better than last time), reduced advantage next, ridden after 3 out, stayed on strongly, benefiting from the return to front-running tactics; he's likeable, straightforward and versatile—with regards ground conditions and type of track—and should go on to give a good account at Aintree next, but the division is wide open this season and he's no certainty to confirm superiority over some of those in behind on another day. **Saphir du Rheu** has done very well since reverted back to hurdling, successful in the Cleeve and running right up to his best on this first foray into an open Grade 1, up against a different Cole Harden this time, under less testing conditions too, obviously handling the good ground fine, but he does go very well in the mud and maybe if he's to improve again in this sphere it'll be on soft/heavy; tracked pace, hit sixth and ninth, ridden after 2 out, chased leader approaching last, stuck to task; given that he's achieved plenty already it's easy to forget how young he is, only a 6-y-o, and although his novice chase season was aborted he does remain quite an exciting prospect for that sphere, whilst if kept hurdling he'd be sure to win more good races. **Zarkandar** is undoubtedly one of the leading staying hurdlers around this season, worth plenty of credit for his consistency even though his win record isn't great over the last 2 seasons, and he shaped well here, unlucky not to finish closer (and possibly even win) after getting the second last all wrong; mid-division, travelled strongly, had made headway to track pace and was going well when bad mistake 2 out, lost place before staying on from last; he was better than the result in the Liverpool Hurdle last season (ridden too aggressively) and seems sure to go well there next month. **At Fishers Cross** has had a really disappointing season overall but got back on track in first-time blinkers (replaced cheekpieces), in the frame for the second successive year; waited with, avoided mistakes, headway under pressure after 2 out, closed all the way to the line and fared best of those held up; he's not sure to be in the same form next time, though. **Whisper** has had a light campaign, presumably not having been quite right all along, and considering this was his first start over hurdles since winning the Grade 1 at Aintree last April it was an encouraging effort, close to his best and shaping as if he'll be sharper for it; raced wide, mid-division, travelled fluently, headway when not fluent 2 out, chased leader approaching last, no extra; the Liverpool Hurdle will presumably be the aim again and he should go well again there. **Un Temps Pour Tout** isn't quite up to the standard required at this level but ran well in a first-time tongue strap 7 weeks after reappearing in the Cleeve; mid-division, travelled well, crept closer seventh, went prominent between last 2, one paced, had every chance; he is a good-looking sort with the size for chasing and will be one to look forward to in that sphere, quite possibly next season.

CHELTENHAM Friday, March 13
GOOD to SOFT (New Course)

JCB Triumph Hurdle (Grade 1) (1) 2m 1f

Pos	Btn	Horse	Age	Wgt	Eq	Trainer	Jockey	SP
1		PEACE AND CO (FR)	4	11-00		Nicky Henderson	Barry Geraghty	2/1f
2	nk	TOP NOTCH (FR)	4	11-00		Nicky Henderson	Daryl Jacob	7/1
3	4	HARGAM (FR)	4	11-00		Nicky Henderson	A. P. McCoy	8/1
4	10	DEVILMENT	4	11-00		John Ferguson	Sam Twiston-Davies	16/1
5	7	PETITE PARISIENNE (FR)	4	10-07		W. P. Mullins, Ireland	Bryan J. Cooper	11/1
6	ns	BELTOR	4	11-00	(h)	Robert Stephens	Tom O'Brien	7/1
7	¾	STARS OVER THE SEA (USA)	4	11-00	(h+t)	David Pipe	Tom Scudamore	50/1
8	½	DICOSIMO (FR)	4	11-00		W. P. Mullins, Ireland	R. Walsh	11/1
9	2¼	OLD GUARD	4	11-00		Paul Nicholls	Nick Scholfield	66/1
10	ns	MATORICO (IRE)	4	11-00		Jonjo O'Neill	Paul Carberry	33/1
11	¾	KAREZAK (IRE)	4	11-00	(b)	Alan King	Wayne Hutchinson	16/1
12	13	PAIN AU CHOCOLAT (FR)	4	11-00		Alan King	Aidan Coleman	16/1
13	hd	PRAIRIE TOWN (IRE)	4	11-00		Tony Carroll	Lee Edwards	150/1
14	3	BARAKA DE THAIX (FR)	4	11-00		David Pipe	Jacques Ricou	40/1
15	26	OFFICER DRIVEL (IRE)	4	11-00	(h)	Jim Best	Noel Fehily	200/1

TIMEFORM'S VIEW | 95

| pu | KALKIR (FR) | 4 | 11-00 | W. P. Mullins, Ireland | P. Townend | 20/1 |

16 ran   Race time: 4m 04.40   Winning Owner: Mr Simon Munir & Mr Isaac Souede

There's been the odd substandard Triumph in recent years, including the 2014 renewal won by Tiger Roll, but that certainly wasn't the case this time around, Peace And Co bettering the performances of all bar Our Conor in the previous 5 years, with each of the first 3—all from the Henderson yard—achieving a level of form at least on a par with recent standards; it was a well-run race—the overall time over a second quicker than for the County Hurdle that followed—and the form overall appeals as very solid. **Peace And Co** marked himself as a most exciting juvenile at Doncaster all the way back in December and underlined the point on a bigger stage this time, maintaining his unbeaten record, and he's a genuinely top-class prospect for the future, potentially Champion Hurdle material, a scopey sort who'll continue to develop physically, whilst mentally he's not yet the finished article either, showing that in the finish here, value for extra; mid-division, tanked along (a bit keener than ideal early on if anything), tracked pace fourth, challenged on bridle before last, led final 100 yds, idled in front but was always holding on; short-term there are further Grade 1 juvenile options at both Aintree and Punchestown and he'd be the one to beat if he took his chance in either. **Top Notch** had done everything asked of him in much calmer waters and more than stepped up to the plate up markedly in grade, confirming himself a very smart, most progressive juvenile and also underlining just what a likeable attitude he has, giving his all to make his talented stablemate work hard; chased leaders, travelled well, hit fifth, edged ahead approaching last, headed final 100 yds, kept on; remains unexposed and is sure to stay at least 2¼m. **Hargam** is improving all the time, not quite a match for his 2 stablemates on the day, but there's a suspicion that the emphasis on stamina was against him and his very best could still be to come; tracked pace, went with enthusiasm, challenged approaching last, not quicken; will prove best at around 2m and appeals as the perfect type for the Anniversary Hurdle at Aintree. **Devilment** ran well upped in grade behind a trio of well-above-average juveniles; mid-division, headway under pressure 2 out, kept on but was no match for the principals; may do better still and could be the sort to be competitive in good-quality handicaps further down the line. **Petite Parisienne** wasn't disgraced but this was a much deeper Grade 1 than she'd won last month and she basically wasn't up to the task; raced wide, tracked pace, untidy 2 out, pushed along soon after, faded. **Beltor** in first-time hood, failed to repeat his impressive Adonis performance but the extra 1f and stiffer track didn't seem an issue and he probably should have finished a bit closer; held up, took strong hold, not fluent fifth, untidy 2 out, hung right, kept on having been left with a lot to do.

Albert Bartlett Novices' Hurdle (Spa) (Grade 1) (1) 3m

Pos	Btn	Horse	Age	Wgt	Eq	Trainer	Jockey	SP
1		MARTELLO TOWER (IRE)	7	11-07		Mrs Margaret Mullins, Ireland	A. P. Heskin	14/1
2	½	MILSEAN (IRE)	6	11-07		W. P. Mullins, Ireland	Daniel Mullins	33/1
3	1	NO MORE HEROES (IRE)	6	11-07		Gordon Elliott, Ireland	Bryan J. Cooper	6/1
4	3¼	ARBRE DE VIE (FR)	5	11-07		W. P. Mullins, Ireland	P. Townend	16/1
5	11	VALUE AT RISK	6	11-07		Dan Skelton	Harry Skelton	8/1
6	2½	SHANTOU BOB (IRE)	7	11-07	(t)	Warren Greatrex	Gavin Sheehan	25/1
7	17	BLACK HERCULES (IRE)	6	11-07		W. P. Mullins, Ireland	R. Walsh	5/2f
8	8	MEASUREOFMYDREAMS (IRE)	7	11-07		W. P. Mullins, Ireland	M. P. Fogarty	100/1
9	10	NATIVE RIVER (IRE)	5	11-07		Colin Tizzard	Brendan Powell	40/1

TIMEFORM'S VIEW

10	3	SHANROE SANTOS (IRE)	6	11-07		Lucy Wadham	Leighton Aspell	100/1
F		OUT SAM	6	11-07		Nicky Henderson	Barry Geraghty	14/1
pu		TEA FOR TWO	6	11-07	(h)	Nick Williams	Lizzie Kelly	18/1
pu		CARNINGLI (IRE)	6	11-07		Rebecca Curtis	Tom Scudamore	66/1
pu		DEFINITLY RED (IRE)	6	11-07		Brian Ellison	Richard Johnson	11/1
pu		THOMAS BROWN	6	11-07	(s)	Harry Fry	Noel Fehily	12/1
pu		BLAKLION	6	11-07		Nigel Twiston-Davies	Sam Twiston-Davies	10/1
pu		CARACCI APACHE (IRE)	5	11-07		Nicky Henderson	Nico de Boinville	20/1
pu		KYLEMORE LOUGH	6	11-07		Richard Lee	Charlie Poste	100/1
pu		AVANT TOUT (FR)	5	11-07		W. P. Mullins, Ireland	D. J. Casey	100/1

19 ran   Race time: 6m 00.30   Winning Owner: Mr Barry Connell

The usual big field assembled for this Grade 1 staying novice and it looks to be a race with plenty of depth to it, lots of them already having shown smart form coming into it, and although not that many coped with a gruelling affair it's certainly form to look upon positively as far as the principals are concerned, the Irish-trained horses dominating, as indeed they have in the novices throughout the meeting; Martello Tower was never far away and the front-running Milsean was headed only in the closing stages, but it wasn't a case of a positional bias looking at how they finished and got so well strung out. **Martello Tower** set the standard on his Limerick win (beat Outlander) and second to the same rival at Leopardstown, a race in which fellow Festival-winners Windsor Park and Killultagh Vic finished behind him, and, although strictly speaking he didn't need to improve to win this most prestigious of staying novices, he's now done it on a bigger stage and was suited by stepping back up in trip, probably helped by the overnight rain too, as he's clearly a strong stayer; prominent, chased leader after 2 out, challenged last, found plenty to lead final 100 yds, driven out, showed a good attitude; he will stay beyond 3m and is a strong, chasing type in appearance, novice chases surely on the cards for 2015/16. **Milsean** hadn't gone on quite as expected from hurdling debut win, turned over twice at short prices since, but had very smart bumper form that suggested he'd be capable of better and delivered it up in grade and trip, the extra 2f no problem at all, seeming to suit in fact; led, went with enthusiasm, shaken up after 2 out, edged right after last, headed final 100 yds by a very strong stayer but kept on well himself; he's a strong, deep-girthed chasing type in appearance and his long-term future no doubt lies over fences. **No More Heroes** produced his best effort yet over jumps, arguably unlucky not to win and certainly worth rating at least alongside the runner-up; mid-division, travelled well, headway approaching 3 out, keeping on when no room before last, lost momentum and switched, then rallied well; this 2f longer trip suited and he's sure to stay beyond 3m, a staying chaser in the making just like the first 2, and he's arguably the best prospect of the lot of them on overall profile. **Arbre de Vie** ran well upped in grade and trip, comfortably his best effort to date, and shaped most of the way as if there'll be an even better performance from him at some point, not such a strong stayer as the placed horses—he'll have no problem dropping back in trip—and also more patiently ridden (did best of those held up); waited with, travelled strongly, good progress after 4 out, went handy before 2 out, driven home turn, one paced; he remains with potential, though worth noting that he's not the biggest if he makes the switch to chasing at any time. **Value At Risk** should ultimately be a strong stayer suited by at least 3m, out of a Midlands Grand

National winner after all, but it's still an early stage of his career and he didn't get home trying 3m for the first time in a well-run championship race on softish ground; raced wide, held up, travelled smoothly, crept closer after halfway, went handy before 2 out, weakened between last 2; he remains a good prospect and will probably go chasing next season. **Shantou Bob** appeared to stay the 3f longer trip, not disgraced in the end, though most of the way he was in last place and there was an element of him passing beaten horses; in rear, jumped none too fluently, some headway after 3 out, plugged on, never on terms. **Black Hercules** hadn't been seen for 3 months, hardly ideal Cheltenham preparation, and despite his strength in the betting he shaped as if needing the run; held up, some headway after 3 out, ridden next, found little.

Betfred Cheltenham Gold Cup Chase (Grade 1) (1) 3m 2f 110y

Pos	Btn	Horse	Age	Wgt	Eq	Trainer	Jockey	SP
1		CONEYGREE	8	11-10		Mark Bradstock	Nico de Boinville	7/1
2	1½	DJAKADAM (FR)	6	11-10		W. P. Mullins, Ireland	R. Walsh	10/1
3	2	ROAD TO RICHES (IRE)	8	11-10		Noel Meade, Ireland	Bryan J. Cooper	8/1
4	6	HOLYWELL (IRE)	8	11-10	(b)	Jonjo O'Neill	Richie McLernon	8/1
5	14	ON HIS OWN (IRE)	11	11-10	(s)	W. P. Mullins, Ireland	Mr P. W. Mullins	33/1
6	1	MANY CLOUDS (IRE)	8	11-10		Oliver Sherwood	Leighton Aspell	7/1
7	2½	SILVINIACO CONTI (FR)	9	11-10	(s)	Paul Nicholls	Noel Fehily	3/1f
8	hd	SMAD PLACE (FR)	8	11-10		Alan King	Wayne Hutchinson	25/1
9	¾	CARLINGFORD LOUGH (IRE)	9	11-10		John E. Kiely, Ireland	A. P. McCoy	14/1
10	14	BOSTON BOB (IRE)	10	11-10		W. P. Mullins, Ireland	P. Townend	33/1
11	ns	HOUBLON DES OBEAUX (FR)	8	11-10		Venetia Williams	Aidan Coleman	33/1
pu		THE GIANT BOLSTER	10	11-10	(h+v)	David Bridgwater	Tom Scudamore	33/1
pu		SAM WINNER (FR)	8	11-10	(s+t)	Paul Nicholls	Sam Twiston-Davies	20/1
pu		BOBS WORTH (IRE)	10	11-10		Nicky Henderson	Barry Geraghty	16/1
pu		HOME FARM (IRE)	8	11-10		Henry de Bromhead, Ireland	D. J. Casey	100/1
pu		LORD WINDERMERE (IRE)	9	11-10		J. Culloty, Ireland	Davy Russell	20/1

16 ran   Race time: 6m 42.70 Closing sectional (3.84f): 60.2s (96.9%)   Winning Owner: The Max Partnership

A terrific field for the 2015 Gold Cup, as intended bringing together the top staying chasers in Britain and Ireland, among them the first 5 from last year and no fewer than 7 in their first season out of novice company, though victory went to one from neither category, front-running Coneygree rewarding his connections' courage in becoming the first novice to win this great race since 1974; a strong gallop on rain-softened ground made for a proper test of stamina and jumping and provided a magnificent spectacle, everything that the season's leading chase should be, each of the first 3 coping admirably well as they pulled clear of the rest after 3 out, the form between them top-class and well up to scratch for a Gold Cup, if not quite at the level of some outstanding renewals over the last decade; it's worth noting the way the race took shape meant there were no hiding places and most had hard races to varying degrees, which needs bearing in mind should any of them show up at Aintree and/or Punchestown. **Coneygree** the first novice even to run in this race since 2006, had rain-softened conditions in his favour and justified the bold call to run here instead of the RSA in becoming the first such horse to win it for more than 40 years, capping a flawless first season over fences with a top-class effort that showcased all his best qualities, a superb display of resolute front-running, expertly handled by a jockey who has only recently ridden out his claim; quickly out in front, he again jumped superbly, quickened an already-strong gallop a circuit out and only had 2 realistic challengers left when shaken up after 3 out, responding most gamely despite edging right on the run-in, seeing out the longer trip thoroughly; this was just his fourth start over fences and the way his career has gone it's easy to believe he may do even better, unlikely to give up his crown lightly back here next year provided he stays sound, likely to be sparingly campaigned in the interim, a clash with the likes of Vautour and Don Poli something to savour. **Djakadam** has found his form taking off since upped to 3m+ and put up the best effort by an Irish-trained staying chaser this season in going down narrowly in his first open Grade 1 chase, coping superbly well with the severe demands of a well-run Gold Cup; travelling strongly and jumping well in mid-field, he edged closer from a circuit out and, having taken third on the home turn, stuck to his task splendidly in pursuit of the winner; a rare 6-y-o to figure in this race, it's possible he'll do even better still and he'll be a fixture in the best staying chases for some time to come, his extraordinary trainer's strength in depth across all divisions at present bordering on the ridiculous. **Road To Riches** ran another stormer 10 weeks on from the Lexus, this an even better effort in form terms, again doing everything right and needing no excuses; close up, jumped soundly, travelled fluently, effort 3 out, kept on, the even longer trip no problem; he's a credit to his trainer and should continue to give a good account. **Holywell** looked well at home in an open Grade 1 chase and ran his race, just not quite good enough in the end but still no mean feat to finish fourth in a Gold Cup, having won handicaps at this meeting in the last 2 seasons, and there are more good races to be won with him over fences; tracked pace, jumped fine, travelled well, shaken up sixteenth, effort before 3 out, one paced straight. **On His Own** ridden by an amateur unable to claim, couldn't match last season's second in this better race but looked in really good nick for most of the way and probably just paid the price for trying to lay up with the gallop set by the winner; close up, jumped right but not markedly so, pushed along 5 out, weakened before 2 out. **Many Clouds** had winning run ended at 3, comfortable for a long way and still looking in good form but maybe just lacking the gears for a demanding, top-class Gold Cup; in touch, jumped fine, shaken up seventeenth, effort 4 out, not quicken next; he's a grand type and will bounce back, even if this probably puts a cap on his potential. **Silviniaco Conti** still just about sets the standard among the staying chasers but wasn't at his best 11 weeks on from the King George, coming up short in this race for the third time, maybe just not cut out for it, the emphasis it places on stamina—particularly with the gallop as it was on softish ground—too much for him, finding uncharacteristically little having gone with zest (if a little keenly) in touch to 4 out; he'll bounce back, and the likes of Aintree, Haydock and Kempton should see him get much closer to the principals another time.

AINTREE Thursday, April 9
GOOD

Betfred Bowl Chase (Grade 1) (1) 3m 1f

Pos	Btn	Horse	Age	Wgt	Eq	Trainer	Jockey	SP
1		SILVINIACO CONTI (FR)	9	11-07	(s)	Paul Nicholls	Noel Fehily	7/4f
2	hd	BALLYNAGOUR (IRE)	9	11-07	(h+t)	David Pipe	Tom Scudamore	18/1
3	2¼	HOLYWELL (IRE)	8	11-07	(b)	Jonjo O'Neill	A. P. McCoy	5/2
4	7	SMAD PLACE (FR)	8	11-07		Alan King	Wayne Hutchinson	10/1
5	14	MENORAH (IRE)	10	11-07		Philip Hobbs	Richard Johnson	7/1

TIMEFORM'S VIEW | 99

6	10	MA FILLEULE (FR)	7	11-00		Nicky Henderson	Daryl Jacob	9/2
pu		VUKOVAR (FR)	6	11-07	(t)	Warren Greatrex	Gavin Sheehan	33/1

7 ran   Race time: 6m 15.60 Closing sectional (3.15f): 46.1s (102.7%)   Winning Owner: Mr Chris Giles & Potensis Bloodstock Ltd

This tends not to be such a deep Grade 1 staying event as others earlier in the campaign but it was a high-quality field of 7 nonetheless, Silviniaco Conti taken on by, amongst others, Gold Cup-fourth Holywell and Ryanair runner-up Ma Filleulle, both of whom were also winners at this meeting in 2014; the winner made all, as he did 12 months earlier, but he set a sound pace, really winding it up early on the final circuit, and although conditions weren't testing it was a good test of both stamina and jumping. **Silviniaco Conti** isn't able to produce his best form at Cheltenham but aside from the Gold Cup he's dominated the Grade 1 staying races in Britain for the last 2 seasons, now a dual winner of Haydock's Betfair Chase, the King George at Kempton and this contest, not needing to be at his very best here but getting the job done under a positive ride—tactics that suit him well these days; he made all of the running, full of enthusiasm and jumping impeccably throughout, and when Fehily had to get more serious after 2 out he responded and just held on; with an exciting crop of novices coming through this season—Coneygree, Vautour and Don Poli in particular—these Grade 1 staying events will be tougher to win next season, but there's little doubt that Silviniaco Conti will continue to make an impact at the flat tracks that suit him so well. **Ballynagour** stands little racing and is rather enigmatic, but on his day he's a very good chaser, as this highlights, comfortably a career-best effort on form in a first-time hood after 4 months off, also proving his stamina for this trip away from testing ground, and, given the fine margin involved, he might well have won but for a blunder 4 out; dropped out, travelled powerfully as usual, smooth headway from thirteenth, bad mistake 4 out, chased leader last and closed all the way to the line, just failing; he goes extremely well fresh and will presumably be primed for either the Betfair Chase or King George first time out next season. **Holywell** again acquitted himself really well, as he had in the Gold Cup, and his record under these sort of conditions in the spring is impossible to knock; prominent, not always fluent, driven 5 out, kept going well, pulled clear of remainder; he's had a light campaign and would be worth considering for Punchestown in a few weeks. **Smad Place** faced a stiff task but did as well as he could under conditions that suited him better than they had in the Gold Cup, though hasn't won this season and could do with sights lowering if he's to get back to winning ways; tracked pace, mistake fourteenth, outpaced 3 out, kept on, no match for principals; he was fifth in the Hennessy but otherwise hasn't been tried in top-end handicaps and they're an option for 2015/16. **Menorah** thrived in the autumn but doesn't hold his form long nowadays and, despite having been kept fresh for this since well held in the King George, he was below form after 3 months off; mid-division, went prominent circuit out, blundered 5 out, struggling next. **Ma Filleule** shaped much better than distance beaten suggests, possibly stretched by the trip (very best form has come at short of 3m), although to find so little it was almost as if there was another problem on the day; tracked pace, travelled well, effort 3 out but folded tamely after next and finished tired. **Vukovar** who had been switched from Harry Fry's stable since last seen 4 months earlier, has a bit to prove given it's so long since he

TIMEFORM'S VIEW

showed his form but is best not judged on this run, out of his depth and up markedly in trip (stays 2¼m); held up, made mistakes, lost touch 5 out, pulled up before last

Doom Bar Aintree Hurdle (Grade 1) (1) 2m 4f

Pos	Btn	Horse	Age	Wgt	Eq	Trainer	Jockey	SP
1		JEZKI (IRE)	7	11-07		Mrs J. Harrington, Ireland	A. P. McCoy	3/1
2	13	ROCK ON RUBY (IRE)	10	11-07	(t)	Harry Fry	Noel Fehily	7/2
3	1½	VOLNAY DE THAIX (FR)	6	11-07		Nicky Henderson	David Bass	8/1
4	6	BLUE HERON (IRE)	7	11-07		Dan Skelton	Harry Skelton	8/1
5	3½	VANITEUX (FR)	6	11-07		Nicky Henderson	Nico de Boinville	16/1
F		ARCTIC FIRE (GER)	6	11-07	(h)	W. P. Mullins, Ireland	R. Walsh	15/8f

6 ran   Race time: 4m 48.20 Closing sectional (3.2f): 46.2s (99.8%)   Winning Owner: Mr John P. McManus

Only 6 runners for this year's Aintree Hurdle but it proved to be a strongly-run affair, Volnay de Thaix and Rock On Ruby racing clear and going hard, and the race was robbed of a good finish when Arctic Fire came down at the final flight; it's not the easiest form to assess but, given neither the second/third were seen to best effect and Jezki was probably booked for second, it's best not to take too high a view. **Jezki** ran without a hood for the first time since before last year's Champion Hurdle win, ridden differently to usual back up in trip too, and, even if he was a fortunate winner with Arctic Fire falling, he seemed in better form than at Cheltenham 4 weeks earlier; dropped out, travelled well, steady headway between 4 out and 3 out, close up 2 out, ridden when left in front last, soon clear as Rock On Ruby was hampered, eased close home; he'll go to Punchestown next, with options at both 2m and 3m, but although connections will probably be keen to explore the longer trip at some stage he's never shaped like a real stayer and isn't bred to be, either. **Rock On Ruby** hadn't been right going into Cheltenham last month so missed that meeting but the reports were positive coming here and he just wasn't seen to best effect under an aggressive ride, even then set to finish close to Jezki only to be impeded by Arctic Fire's last-flight fall; pressed leader at strong pace, went with zest, led 2 out, headed approaching last, badly hampered there, no extra. **Volnay de Thaix** faced a stiff task in this grade but shaped as if still in good form under an overly-aggressive ride; forced pace, ridden when headed 2 out, weakening when left in a place last. **Arctic Fire** has got better and better as the season's gone on, and he looked set to win his first Grade 1 here only to meet the last all wrong and crash out; waited with, travelled powerfully, hit 4 out, good progress soon after, tracked pace 3 out, edged ahead approaching last, yet to be asked for effort when fell heavily there, going best at time and likely to have won for all that his stamina wasn't proven over this 3f longer trip; he got up okay soon after but may need time to recover from this before a likely Flat campaign which his trainer had mentioned after Cheltenham.

AINTREE Friday, April 10
GOOD

E-Lites Top Novices' Hurdle (Grade 2) (1) 2m 110y

Pos	Btn	Horse	Age	Wgt	Eq	Trainer	Jockey	SP
1		CYRUS DARIUS	6	11-04		Malcolm Jefferson	Brian Hughes	8/1
2	10	VAGO COLLONGES (FR)	6	11-04	(t)	Paul Nicholls	Sam Twiston-Davies	7/1
3	1¾	QEWY (IRE)	5	11-04		John Ferguson	A. P. McCoy	5/1
4	10	GLINGERBURN (IRE)	7	11-04		Nicky Richards	Brian Harding	7/4f
5	1½	CARDINAL WALTER (IRE)	6	11-04	(h)	Nicky Henderson	Andrew Tinkler	8/1
6	30	JOLLY'S CRACKED IT (FR)	6	11-04		Harry Fry	Noel Fehily	8/1

TIMEFORM'S VIEW | 101

7	10	MONTDRAGON (FR)	5	11-04	(t)	Jonjo O'Neill	Richie McLernon	50/1
8	17	TRADER JACK	6	11-04		David Flood	Stephen Craine	100/1
9	ds	DABADIYAN (IRE)	5	11-04		Gary Moore	Joshua Moore	66/1
F		ENDLESS CREDIT (IRE)	5	11-04	(t)	Micky Hammond	Joe Colliver	25/1
ur		COMMISSIONED (IRE)	5	11-04		John Ferguson	Richard Johnson	10/1

11 ran   Race time: 3m 59.80 Closing sectional (3.2f): 45.5s (102.2%)   Winning Owner: Mr & Mrs G Calder & Mr P M Warren

Even though disappointing efforts from the likes of Glingerburn and Jolly's Cracked It made this a bit weaker there was an improver that stepped up to the mark in Cyrus Darius, putting up a near high-class effort, and the placed pair are ones with solid efforts to their name in similar events this season, giving the form some substance; it was a reasonably well-run race courtesy of the free-going Endless Credit and tactics didn't seem crucial. **Cyrus Darius** has quickly come a very long way, not making his hurdling debut until last month, and marked himself down as not only one of this season's top novice hurdlers but a truly exciting horse for the future as he overcame a steep rise in class in style, ahead of talented opponents who had the benefit of more experience; raced in mid-field, travelled powerfully and jumped fine, headway 3 out, led on bridle soon after next and forged clear when Brian Hughes got after him; this was most impressive in every respect and he remains with plenty of potential, including for chasing, as he's certainly built to jump a fence. **Vago Collonges** who ran without the hood this time, has won only once in his novice hurdle campaign but has kept good company right the way through and deserves credit for his consistency; prominent, travelled well, went on after sixth, untidy 2 out, headed soon after, one paced, no match for winner; although he's not progressing at this stage his strong-travelling style gives hope there could yet be a bit more in the locker and he strikes as the type that'll be well suited by the nature of big-field handicaps—a BHA mark of 141 coming into this is by no means prohibitive. **Qewy** hasn't progressed any further on form since Newbury win but his efforts in both the Supreme and this have been creditable and it shouldn't be forgotten that he's only 4 races into his hurdling career; held up, travelled well, headway 3 out, close up next, edged left, not quicken. **Glingerburn** is much better than this, highly progressive to this point and little reason to knock his form, the emphasis here possibly more on speed than is absolutely ideal—his last 2 wins and best performances have been over 2f further on soft ground—but even allowing for that he looked rather laboured; mid-division, ridden before 3 out, just plugged on and was never a win threat; a break will probably do him the world of good and he remains one to look forward to next season, when a switch to fences could be on the cards. **Cardinal Walter** faced by far his stiffest task to date over hurdles and, though not disgraced, failed to produce his best form; chased leaders, effort 3 out, held between last 2, no extra; he's in excellent hands and is worth another chance having created a good impression previously. **Jolly's Cracked It** clearly wasn't 100% on the day and is better judged on previous form; chased leaders, lost place after 4 out, folded, eased off; he may benefit from a break now and could still make an impact in good-quality handicap hurdles next season. **Montdragon** on first outing since leaving E. Leenders (runner-up only start over hurdles in France) and in a tongue strap after 10 months off, was flying too high in this grade; raced off the pace, struggling 4 out, never landed a blow; remains unexposed and will no doubt face much easier tasks ahead.

Betfred Mildmay Novices' Chase (Grade 1) (1) 3m 1f

Pos	Btn	Horse	Age	Wgt	Eq	Trainer	Jockey	SP
1		SAPHIR DU RHEU (FR)	6	11-04		Paul Nicholls	Sam Twiston-Davies	13/8f
2	15	CARRAIG MOR (IRE)	7	11-04		Alan King	Noel Fehily	12/1
3	hd	IRISH SAINT (FR)	6	11-04	(t)	Paul Nicholls	Nick Scholfield	6/1
4	23	WAKANDA (IRE)	6	11-04		Sue Smith	Sean Quinlan	40/1
5	11	CAROLE'S DESTRIER	7	11-04		Neil Mulholland	A. P. McCoy	4/1
6	28	AINSI FIDELES (FR)	5	11-04	(b+t)	David Pipe	Tom Scudamore	9/1
F		RAWNAQ (IRE)	8	11-04		Matthew J. Smith, Ireland	A. E. Lynch	20/1
F		IRISH CAVALIER (IRE)	6	11-04	(s)	Rebecca Curtis	P. Townend	8/1
pu		CLOSE TOUCH	7	11-04		Nicky Henderson	David Bass	14/1

9 ran   Race time: 6m 19.00   Closing sectional (3.15f): 49.2s (97.1%)   Winning Owner: The Stewart Family

Although this wasn't the deepest of fields for a Grade 1 novice chase, lacking any of the stars from Cheltenham, it still involved a host of smart types with solid form and Saphir du Rheu, who'd finished second in the World Hurdle last month, ran out a wide-margin winner, producing one of the best performances in this race in recent years—no mean feat when it's been won by the likes of Silviniaco Conti, Dynaste and Holywell. **Saphir du Rheu** has had a stop-start novice chase campaign but emphatically answered any questions there were with regards his jumping of fences with a flawless display back in this sphere, proving himself every bit as good a chaser as he is hurdler, and there's an expectancy that he'll do better still next season; he was ridden confidently by Sam Twiston-Davies, positive on him from the start, racing close up, full of exhuberance and jumping boldly, and after taking it up 4 out the result was never in doubt, drawing clear between the last 2 fences, eased a tad close home and most impressive; there are a whole host of very exciting novice chasers to look forward to in the top open races next season, Saphir du Rheu absolutely one of them, and he'll merit the utmost respect wherever he goes next. **Carraig Mor** had a mid-season blip but has generally progressed well over fences and this was the best effort of his career so far, beaten only by a high-class opponent and worth credit for pushing Saphir du Rheu for as long as he did, the only one that was able to; prominent, jumped well in main and went with enthusiasm, led fifth, headed 4 out, held when mistake 2 out, finished tired; he can do better still next season. **Irish Saint** seemed to be stretched by the 3f longer trip, even though he was pressing Carraig Mor (who'd been positively ridden and was getting tired) for second at the line, and shaped as if still in top form; patiently ridden, travelled smoothly, steady headway from 5 out, chased leaders 3 out, appeared Saphir du Rheu's main threat at that point but found a bit less than looked likely; he's likely to prove best up to an easy 3m and not out of the question that he shows better form as a second-season chaser, a valuable handicap such as the Paddy Power Gold Cup probably worth considering. **Wakanda** wasn't disgraced considering the stiff task he faced; chased leaders, ridden when blundered 5 out, left behind soon after but plugged on to hit the frame; he gives the impression that he's likely to stay long distances. **Carole's Destrier** was entitled to a crack at this higher grade but produced a laboured effort, perhaps just a sign that he's ready for a break; led until fifth, driven twelfth (off bridle before most), lost touch 4 out.

Betfred Melling Chase (Grade 1) (1) 2m 4f

Pos	Btn	Horse	Age	Wgt	Eq	Trainer	Jockey	SP
1		DON COSSACK (GER)	8	11-10	(t)	Gordon Elliott, Ireland	A. P. McCoy	3/1jf
2	26	CUE CARD	9	11-10		Colin Tizzard	Daryl Jacob	6/1
3	4½	JOHNS SPIRIT (IRE)	8	11-10		Jonjo O'Neill	Richie McLernon	16/1

TIMEFORM'S VIEW | 103

4	1¾	CHAMPAGNE FEVER (IRE)	8	11-10		W. P. Mullins, Ireland	R. Walsh	3/1jf
5	3¾	AL FEROF (FR)	10	11-10		Paul Nicholls	Sam Twiston-Davies	11/2
6	9	SIMPLY NED (IRE)	8	11-10		Nicky Richards	Brian Harding	25/1
7	30	WISHFULL THINKING	12	11-10	(t)	Philip Hobbs	Richard Johnson	25/1
F		SIRE DE GRUGY (FR)	9	11-10		Gary Moore	Joshua Moore	8/1
F		BALDER SUCCES (FR)	7	11-10		Alan King	Wayne Hutchinson	8/1
pu		CROCO BAY (IRE)	8	11-10		Ben Case	Kielan Woods	33/1

10 ran   Race time: 4m 52.30 Closing sectional (3.15f): 46.8s (98.4%)   Winning Owner: Gigginstown House Stud

A vintage field on paper for this year's Melling Chase, no fewer than 6 of the 10 established as top class, though most had something to prove as well and in the event there were more disappointing runs that good ones; as such, the form isn't the easiest to assess, with a bit of an end-of-season feel, though even a conservative view has the winner putting up a tip-top effort, and the visual impression in a well-run race was about as positive as it gets. **Don Cossack** wasted no time making amends for his unlucky defeat in the Ryanair, putting up a top-class effort to turn a Grade 1 into such a procession, potentially one of the best over fences anywhere in recent seasons, even taking into account that most of his obvious rivals underperformed; racing close up, he always looked comfortable in a well-run race, jumped superbly and surged right away from floundering rivals after being produced to lead 3 out; the Grade 1 chase scene at this trip and beyond is something to savour, especially with this season's excellent crop of novices about to step up, and Don Cossack is going to be a major player whatever the opposition. **Cue Card** went with plenty of zest 4 months on from when last seen in the King George but had no answer when tackled by the winner, evidence mounting that his problems over the last couple of seasons mean he's just not the top-class chaser of old; made running, travelled well, joined 4 out, headed when mistake next, no extra from 2 out. **Johns Spirit** shaped similarly to last time in another Grade 1, in good nick but not up to the task; mid-division, headway tenth, in touch when ridden before 3 out, no extra from next. **Champagne Fever** closely matched with the winner judged on Thurles form in January, was well backed but ran below form after 8 weeks off, having been forced to miss Cheltenham, not asked to lead this time and not picking up having raced in mid-field to 4 out, a mistake at the next finishing him off.

AINTREE Saturday, April 11
GOOD

Silver Cross Stayers' Hurdle (Liverpool) (Grade 1) (1) 3m 110y

Pos	Btn	Horse	Age	Wgt	Eq	Trainer	Jockey	SP
1		WHISPER (FR)	7	11-07		Nicky Henderson	Nico de Boinville	5/1
2	3½	COLE HARDEN (IRE)	6	11-07	(t)	Warren Greatrex	Gavin Sheehan	2/1f
3	6	UN TEMPS POUR TOUT (IRE)	6	11-07	(b+t)	David Pipe	Tom Scudamore	15/2
4	11	ZARKANDAR (IRE)	8	11-07	(b+t)	Paul Nicholls	Sam Twiston-Davies	5/2
5	28	HENRYVILLE	7	11-07	(h)	Harry Fry	Noel Fehily	12/1
6	3	BROTHER BRIAN (IRE)	7	11-07		Hughie Morrison	Tom O'Brien	20/1
7	2	CRACK AWAY JACK	11	11-07		Emma Lavelle	Aidan Coleman	25/1
pu		JETSON (IRE)	10	11-07		Mrs J. Harrington, Ireland	R. Walsh	11/1
pu		BLUE FASHION (IRE)	6	11-07		Nicky Henderson	David Bass	28/1

9 ran   Race time: 5m 58.30 Closing sectional (3.15f): 47.2s (97.6%)   Winning Owner: Walters Plant Hire Ltd

A good, competitive renewal of this Grade 1 staying event, featuring the winner and third from the World Hurdle in Cole Harden and Zarkandar as well as Whisper, who won this race 12 months ago and had shaped well behind that pair in fifth at Cheltenham last month; it was a strongly-run affair, Cole Harden if anything ridden a tad too aggressively, and they were strung out from the start, none of the outsiders ever landing a blow. **Whisper** has had a light campaign, only 2 runs since winning this corresponding event 12 months ago, so it's understandable that the World Hurdle might have come a bit too soon for him to be right at his best and he confirmed the promise of that Cheltenham run to win this again with an even better performance than in 2014; mid-division, travelled well, went prominent eighth, ridden 3 out, led approaching next, responded well to assert; he was suited by the way the race developed, with the runner-up setting a strong pace, but certainly not flattered in any way and, with another crack at chasing seeming unlikely in the short term, he'll surely be a contender for all of the top staying hurdles next season for all that it'll be worth remembering that he's probably not the easiest to train. **Cole Harden** didn't quite follow up his World Hurdle win in another Grade 1 but put up a bold show nonetheless to more or less confirm the improvement from Cheltenham, worth some extra credit this day too, asked to do a bit too much too soon; forced pace, went with zest, mistake seventh, really pressed on after next, headed approaching 2 out, kept on as best he could but unable to fight back at more patiently-ridden Whisper; he's thoroughly genuine and likeable and can win more of these top staying hurdles. **Un Temps Pour Tout** falls a little short of the very best in this division, that much clear after defeats in the Cleeve, World Hurdle and this, but each time he's given a good account, with blinkers fitted here, and it's praiseworthy that he's consistently showing very smart form in top company; chased leaders, ridden before 3 out, kept on, had every chance; he ran really well in a handicap at Punchestown last year and has the 3m Grade 1 at the same meeting as a likely target this time around. **Zarkandar** looked to have a lot in his favour, conditions ideal, but was rather disappointing, the World Hurdle possibly having taken the edge off him slightly (does seem to go particularly well fresh nowadays), although a blunder at a crucial point in the race no doubt contributed to a below-par run as well; chased leaders, bad mistake 5 out as things were really starting to take shape, ridden before 3 out, held 2 out, no extra final 100 yds; he should bounce back in other similar events, particularly after a break, some of the French races he contested in 2014 likely to be targets again.

PUNCHESTOWN Wednesday, April 29
GOOD to SOFT

Bibby Financial Services Ireland Punchestown Gold Cup Chase (Grade 1) 3m 1f

Pos	Btn	Horse	Age	Wgt	Eq	Trainer	Jockey	SP
1		DON COSSACK (GER)	8	11-10	(t)	Gordon Elliott, Ireland	Paul Carberry	5/2
2	7	DJAKADAM (FR)	6	11-10		W. P. Mullins, Ireland	R. Walsh	2/1f
3	6½	ROAD TO RICHES (IRE)	8	11-10		Noel Meade, Ireland	Bryan J. Cooper	4/1
4	2	CUE CARD	9	11-10	(s+t)	Colin Tizzard	Aidan Coleman	12/1
5	24	BOSTON BOB (IRE)	10	11-10		W. P. Mullins, Ireland	D. J. Casey	16/1
F		THE GIANT BOLSTER	10	11-10	(b)	David Bridgwater	Tom Cannon	33/1
F		BALLYNAGOUR (IRE)	9	11-10	(h+t)	David Pipe	Tom Scudamore	9/1
pu		ON HIS OWN (IRE)	11	11-10	(s)	W. P. Mullins, Ireland	P. Townend	14/1

8 ran   Race time: 6m 21.50 Closing sectional (3.55f): 50.4s (107.5%)   Winning Owner: Gigginstown House Stud

No Cheltenham Gold Cup winner but there was the second and third best thing with Djakadam and Road To Riches in opposition, and their presence drew another top-class effort from Don Cossack, one that would have won him the chasing blue riband last month

TIMEFORM'S VIEW

had he gone for it instead of the Ryanair, this display cementing the winner's status as the best staying chaser around on Timeform ratings—it's likely the most potent threats to that mantle lie in the novice ranks rather than the more established order; the pace was fair, Road To Riches forcing it for most of the way. **Don Cossack** has completely come of age, unrecognisable from the horse well beaten in the novice at this meeting in 2014, delivering the goods on the biggest stage on his last 2 starts, a luckless run in the Ryanair the only thing that's prevented a clean sweep at the major spring Festivals; ridden more patiently, presumably due to the longer trip, he jumped well bar leaping into the back of On His Own at the eleventh and, having made his effort wide of the second/third on the home turn, found plenty to get on top between the last 2, forging clear, proving his stamina for this sort of test in no uncertain terms and giving every indication the extra distance of the Cheltenham Gold Cup won't be a problem, either—indeed, he's categorically the staying chaser that the likes of Don Poli and Vautour (not to mention reigning champion Coneygree) now have to aim at. **Djakadam** ran his heart out in defeat at the top level for the second start in a row, confirming Cheltenham superiority over Road To Riches by a greater margin but running into an even tougher opponent than Coneygree as it happened, this performance as good if not better; jumping boldly close up, he travelled so well he went to the front briefly at the seventh and edged ahead again after 2 out, only for Don Cossack to take his measure approaching the last; it's worth reiterating he's still only 6, sure to win more good races in 2015/16. **Road To Riches** perhaps dipped a little below his Cheltenham form but shaped as if still in good heart, entirely possible he just hadn't recovered from that gruelling race so well as Djakadam, even 7 weeks on; led, headed briefly seventh, ridden when joined again home turn, rallied until last, no extra; it's only going to get tougher to take gain revenge on the 2-year younger runner-up, let alone Don Cossack and Coneygree, but there are bound to be several winning openings for him in 2015/16. **Cue Card** clearly still has something to offer judged on both this and Aintree, not impossible he takes his revival up another notch whilst accepting he'll almost certainly never scale the heights he managed pre-injury, seeing things out in a far more satisfactory manner in first-time cheekpieces and tongue strap here despite stepping back up in trip, likely also he's better ridden more positively than he was on the day; typically took strong hold in touch, shuffled back briefly 5 out, ridden in fourth approaching straight, one paced straight but closed gap on fading Road To Riches late on.

PUNCHESTOWN Thursday, April 30
GOOD to SOFT

Ladbrokes World Series Hurdle (Grade 1) 3m

Pos	Btn	Horse	Age	Wgt	Eq	Trainer	Jockey	SP
1		JEZKI (IRE)	7	11-10		Mrs J. Harrington, Ireland	M. P. Walsh	5/2
2	1¾	HURRICANE FLY (IRE)	11	11-10		W. P. Mullins, Ireland	R. Walsh	6/4f
3	8	ZABANA (IRE)	6	11-10		Andrew Lynch, Ireland	J. J. Burke	20/1
4	3¾	LIEUTENANT COLONEL	6	11-10		Ms Sandra Hughes, Ireland	Bryan J. Cooper	7/1
5	3½	TTEBBOB (IRE)	6	11-10	(h)	Mrs J. Harrington, Ireland	Robbie Power	28/1
6	½	JETSON (IRE)	10	11-10		Mrs J. Harrington, Ireland	Davy Russell	14/1
7	2½	THOUSAND STARS (FR)	11	11-10	(s)	W. P. Mullins, Ireland	P. Townend	9/1
8	1¾	ZAIDPOUR (FR)	9	11-10	(s)	W. P. Mullins, Ireland	D. J. Casey	33/1
9	3¼	CAPTAINOFTHEFLEET (IRE)	8	11-10		Eamon O'Connell, Ireland	Mr E. O'Connell	66/1

TIMEFORM'S VIEW

| 10 | 16 | LOTS OF MEMORIES (IRE) | 8 | 11-10 | | P. G. Fahey, Ireland | P. D. Kennedy | 33/1 |
| 11 | ds | I SHOT THE SHERIFF (IRE) | 8 | 11-10 | (t) | A. J. Martin, Ireland | Paul Carberry | 12/1 |

11 ran Race time: 5m 52.10 Closing sectional (4.3f): 60s (105.1%) Winning Owner: Mr John P. McManus

A fascinating renewal of this Grade 1, featuring 2 previous winners of the Champion Hurdle, both of whom were trying this trip for the first time, and they duly fought out the finish, Jezki getting the better of the argument on this occasion to follow in the footsteps of his half-brother, Jetson, who took this prize last year; it was run at a fair pace. **Jezki** seems to come good at this time of year and belied any fears about the longer trip to win at this meeting for the third successive year, turning around form from earlier in the season with Hurricane Fly in the process, not needing to improve upon a somewhat fortuitous win at Aintree to claim his eighth victory at this level; held up, travelled strongly, produced to lead approaching last, driven out; beaten on all 4 starts at around 2m since successful in the Champion Hurdle here last year, including when no match for Faugheen at Cheltenham, it seems likely that he will be kept to this sort of trip. **Hurricane Fly** has enjoyed another highly productive campaign and lost little in defeat on his first try at further than 2½m, lack of stamina not to blame, keeping on in typically game fashion but just unable to reel in his old adversary Jezki; mid-division, lost place early final circuit, headway 3 out, ridden next, stuck to task; a wonderfully tough and consistent performer, he is likely to take plenty of beating if sent for the French Champion Hurdle at Auteuil, but it remains to be seen if that will be his swansong. **Zabana** coped well with the step up in grade, fully confirming the improvement shown in the Coral Cup last time; chased leaders, ridden before 2 out, stayed on without threatening the first 2; a rangy sort, he looks the type to do well over fences next season should connections opt to go down that route. **Lieutenant Colonel** without the headgear this time, settled and ran better than in the World Hurdle but appears to have reached his limit in this sphere; prominent, ridden after 3 out, faded straight; a return to chasing is on the cards and is open to improvement over the larger obstacles.

TIMEFORM'S BEST OF 2014/15

The single biggest story of the 2014/15 season was a human rather than an equine one. A. P. McCoy announced in February, immediately after reaching two hundred winners for the ninth time in his career on Mr Mole in the Game Spirit, that he would retire at the end of the season upon securing his twentieth Champion Jockey title. From then on the whole season was seemingly framed around McCoy's farewell roadshow, with added attention put upon his final Festival winner (**Uxizandre** (c168) in the Ryanair Chase) and his ride in the National, Shutthefrontdoor, who ultimately went off 6/1 favourite and looked the likeliest winner for a long way before fading into fifth.

Besides the due reverence for McCoy, the 2014/15 season contained more than its share of quality performances and rare achievements. A novice won the Cheltenham Gold Cup, but wasn't even Timeform's Champion Novice Chaser; the Hennessy-Grand National double was completed for the first time; and a Grade 1 record that could stand for decades was set by another retiring great. Performances by the season's novices, both over fences and hurdles, were truly remarkable and set up a hotly-anticipated winter across all four of the main divisions.

Staying Chasers

It's unlikely that anyone has forgotten the defining image of the chasing campaign, and arguably the whole National Hunt season. Novice **Coneygree**'s (c170p) success in the Cheltenham Gold Cup for the unheralded Mark Bradstock yard was one of the most heartening big-race outcomes for some time. Like that other great Gold Cup of recent years, the 2011 renewal won by Long Run, it signalled a sudden power shift at the top of the division—not just in terms of the winner this time, as second-season chasers **Djakadam** (c170) and **Road To Riches** (c167) filled the places.

Like Long Run, who lost out to a resurgent Kauto Star in the following season's Betfair Chase and King George, the new order may not have things all their own way. There's the extraordinary fact that Coneygree wasn't even Timeform's leading novice chaser last season (more on that below), but there's also an emergent threat whose talent and stamina is only now starting to bear the long-promised fruit. **Don Cossack** (c180)

Don Cossack leads over the last in the Punchestown Gold Cup

ended 2014/15 as Timeform's highest-rated jumper in training, following thumping successes in both the Melling Chase and the Punchestown Gold Cup, on the latter occasion having Djakadam and Road To Riches significantly further behind than Coneygree managed at Cheltenham.

It would also be too soon to write off certain members of the old guard. **Silviniaco Conti** (c172) looked imperious either side of Cheltenham, sweeping up the Betfair Chase and King George before gaining recompense for another Gold Cup disappointment in Aintree's Bowl. It was also a breakthrough year for **Menorah** (c169), who won the Charlie Hall and finished second in the Betfair Chase before taking the Oaksey Chase on the final day of the season. Though rising eleven now, he should be a player again in 2015/16, as should King George runner-up **Dynaste** (c167), who missed Cheltenham and Aintree after sustaining an injury in the BetBright Cup (Cotswold Chase). That race was won by Hennessy winner **Many Clouds** (c168), who of course went on to take the Grand National. Though up to competing in open graded contests, Many Clouds will probably have his campaign geared around a bid to become the first winner of back-to-back Nationals since Red Rum in the 1970s.

Two-mile Chasers

All the buzz in this division at the beginning of the season surrounded the return of **Sprinter Sacre** (c163), whose imperious, era-defining best in 2012/13 remained fresh in the mind even after his lengthy absence. Sprinter Sacre reappeared in the Clarence House at Ascot on January, and initially his second to the match-fit **Dodging Bullets** (c168), who had already beaten **Somersby** (c165) in the Tingle Creek in December, gave his followers plenty of encouragement going into the Champion Chase, especially after **Sire de Grugy**'s (c168) early-season injury woes.

Sire de Grugy would eventually reappear in the Game Spirit at Newbury in February, where he looked rusty and eventually unseated Jamie Moore three out, allowing the reformed **Mr Mole** (c160) to pick up the pieces. Sire de Grugy got back to winning ways two weeks later at Chepstow, but his rushed preparation for the defence of his Cheltenham crown was evident, and he was below his best in the Champion Chase, as was Sprinter Sacre, who was pulled up after jumping three out. With the two former winners underperforming, it was Dodging Bullets once again who took advantage, confirming himself the best of the established two-milers in completing a Grade 1 hat-trick as he beat old-hand Somersby and breakthrough performer (won Desert Orchid and Celebration Chase) **Special Tiara** (c167). Dodging Bullets wasn't Timeform's highest-rated two-mile chaser in 2014/15, though, with that honour going to runaway Arkle winner **Un de Sceaux** (c169p), who has accordingly been ante-post favourite for the 2016 Champion Chase pretty much since the market was formed.

Novice Chasers

It is a testament to the strength of the division that **Coneygree**—the first novice to win the Cheltenham Gold Cup since Captain Christy in 1974, nor the above-mentioned **Un de Sceaux**—finished the season as Timeform's highest-rated novice chaser. That honour goes to **Vautour** (c171p). Vautour had produced one of the most stunning performances of the 2014 Cheltenham Festival when spread-eagling his rivals in the Supreme Novices' Hurdle, and he once again rather stole the show in 2015, putting up the most visually-impressive performance of the week—and the best in terms of ratings—when beating Grade 1-winning chasers **Apache Stronghold** (c153) and **Valseur Lido** (c155) by fifteen lengths in the JLT Novices' Chase. Sent into the lead from the outset, Vautour jumped superbly, travelled strongly and was always in command, routing his rivals with a top-class performance.

Coneygree has already been touched upon in the staying chasers section, and it goes without saying that last year's Gold Cup winner will once again be a formidable force, particularly when stamina is at a premium. The likes of RSA Chase winner **Don Poli** (c161p) and Mildmay Novices' Chase winner **Saphir du Rheu** (c161p) will add further

The imperious Un de Sceaux

lustre to a fascinating staying-chase scene, with both horses certainly possessing the potential to cut it at the highest level in open company.

Debate will continue to rage about which of last season's novice chasers was the best, though it surely cannot be argued that Un de Sceaux wasn't the best at two miles. A casualty on his chasing bow at Gowran, Un de Sceaux won his four subsequent starts in dominant fashion, three of those wins achieved at the highest level, and he will take all the beating in open company over two miles this season.

Other horses worthy of note include **Sizing Granite** (c155p)—the beneficiary of Un de Sceaux bypassing Aintree's Maghull Novices' Chase—and the mare **Vroum Vroum Mag** (c151P), who is unbeaten in five starts over fences and looks one of the brightest prospects around.

Staying Hurdlers

With 2014 World Hurdle winner **More of That** (h170 in 2013/14) not seen again after flopping in the Long Distance Hurdle at Newbury in November and runner-up **Annie Power** (h162) aimed at the David Nicholson Mares' Hurdle instead, the staying hurdle division was more open than ever, as was manifested by the spread of different big-race winners through the season.

Medinas (h153) rather stole the Long Distance Hurdle from **Cole Harden** (h164) who, after a breathing operation, went on to put up the best performance of the season when making all in the World Hurdle. Cleeve Hurdle winner **Saphir du Rheu** (h161) was second and **Zarkandar** (h160), a Group 1 winner in France in the autumn, third after getting the second-last all wrong. It was another near-miss for Zarkandar, who had travelled all over **Reve de Sivola** (h159) in the Long Walk at Ascot before that one rallied gamely to take the race for the third successive year.

Whisper (h163) emerged as potentially the biggest challenger to Cole Harden, beating him in Aintree's Liverpool Hurdle after an abortive chasing campaign. Further spice was added to the division when former Champion Hurdler **Jezki** (h168) stepped up to three miles to win the World Series Hurdle at Punchestown, where he beat old rival **Hurricane Fly** (h167), though Jezki has been ruled out of the 2015/16 season through injury; **Un Temps Pour Tout** (h162) stepped up on his British form when a ten-length winner of the Grande Course de Haies at Auteuil in June from a field that included Zarkandar and Hurricane Fly. With few guarantees about which of this season's crop will stay hurdling or switch to fences, this division looks to remain the most open ahead of the new season.

Two-mile Hurdlers

There was also transition in the two-mile hurdling division, though this one was a lot smoother and more decisive. Dual Champion Hurdler **Hurricane Fly** took the twentieth, twenty-first and twenty-second Grade 1 of his career in Ireland over the winter, getting the better of defending Champion Hurdle winner Jezki each time. When it came to the latest Champion, however, he could finish only third, behind two stablemates four and five years his junior respectively, **Faugheen** (h171+) and **Arctic Fire** (h168).

Faugheen is the natural heir to Hurricane Fly and was the outstanding two-mile hurdler of the season. He maintained his flawless record throughout the campaign, taking the Ascot Hurdle and the Christmas Hurdle at Kempton with ease before returning in the spring to win the Champion Hurdle at Cheltenham and its Punchestown equivalent. He is now ten from ten under Rules and, still just seven, he looks the biggest immediate threat to his predecessor's Grade 1 record.

Faugheen is likely to face some new faces this term. As well as the retirement of Hurricane Fly in late-summer, International Hurdle winner **The New One** (h166) could be set for a step up in trip after being run off his feet in the Champion, while **Jezki** has been ruled out for the season. Only **My Tent Or Yours** (h168), the Champion Hurdle

The unbeaten Faugheen leads home his stablemates Arctic Fire and Hurricane Fly (hidden) in the Champion Hurdle

runner-up in 2014 who missed last season due to injury, remains of the old guard, along with Arctic Fire, who is overdue a first Grade 1 success after three second-placed finishes last season. He looked set to win the Aintree Hurdle before crashing out at the last and handing the race to Jezki.

Novice Hurdlers (including Juveniles)

The Rich Ricci-owned, Willie Mullins-trained duo of Faugheen and Vautour dominated the novice hurdle division in the 2013/14 season, and the same connections were responsible for the outstanding performer in the latest campaign as **Douvan** (h168p) stamped himself as a horse of the highest calibre. Douvan was successful on all four starts after joining Willie Mullins from France, the undoubted highlight coming in the Supreme Novices' Hurdle at the Festival, in which he put up one of the best performances in the race's history.

Douvan went to Punchestown as opposed to Aintree, which left the door open for **Cyrus Darius** (h159p) to announce himself as a very exciting prospect in the Top Novices' Hurdle. The Malcolm Jefferson-trained gelding had gone under the radar somewhat having not contested a graded hurdle prior to Aintree, but he handed out a ten-length beating to some rivals with solid form, earning a rating second only to Douvan amongst the non-juvenile novice hurdlers.

Nicky Henderson-trained juvenile hurdlers **Peace And Co** (h161P) and **Top Notch** (160), first and second respectively in the Triumph Hurdle, achieved higher ratings than Cyrus Darius, with stablemate **Hargam** (154) completing a famous one-two-three for the yard. Peace And Co has run just three times for Henderson and, as can be seen elsewhere in this book, is a tremendous prospect who looks the main threat to Faugheen for the 2016 Champion Hurdle.

Windsor Park (h154p) and **Martello Tower** (h155) won the Neptune and Albert Bartlett respectively at Cheltenham and both have bright futures, presumably over longer trips. Another who still has more to offer is **Nichols Canyon** (h156p), who won at both Aintree and Punchestown.

HORSES TO FOLLOW
2014/15 STATISTICS

TRAINERS (1,2,3 earnings)		Horses	Indiv'l Wnrs	Races Won	Runs	% Strike Rate	Stakes £
1	Paul Nicholls	139	73	124	517	24.0	3,128,873
2	Nicky Henderson	156	82	129	499	25.9	1,793,517
3	Philip Hobbs	136	71	102	551	18.5	1,435,431
4	W. P. Mullins, Ireland	63	13	16	91	17.6	1,309,857
5	David Pipe	136	67	116	579	20.0	1,176,751
6	Alan King	121	49	75	448	16.7	1,045,054
7	Oliver Sherwood	56	20	31	204	15.2	1,023,874
8	Jonjo O'Neill	165	70	104	634	16.4	876,894
9	Nigel Twiston-Davies	117	49	73	487	15.0	821,665
10	Venetia Williams	112	41	53	441	12.0	791,622

JOCKEYS (by winners)		1st	2nd	3rd	Unpl	Total Rides	% Strike Rate
1	A. P. McCoy	231	149	110	337	827	27.9
2	Richard Johnson	153	164	120	422	859	17.8
3	Tom Scudamore	150	100	83	352	685	21.9
4	Sam Twiston-Davies	145	118	99	396	758	19.1
5	Brian Hughes	106	94	82	372	654	16.2
6	Noel Fehily	85	63	82	247	477	17.8
7	Aidan Coleman	82	78	81	412	653	12.6
8	Gavin Sheehan	73	47	42	239	401	18.2
9	Paul Moloney	72	64	70	326	532	13.5
10	Paddy Brennan	67	64	50	261	442	15.2

SIRES OF WINNERS (1,2,3 earnings)		Races Won	Runs	% Strike Rate	Stakes £
1	King's Theatre (by Sadler's Wells)	148	753	19.7	1,724,177
2	Milan (by Sadler's Wells)	110	740	14.9	1,237,399
3	Presenting (by Mtoto)	136	883	15.4	1,214,178
4	Kayf Tara (by Sadler's Wells)	108	861	12.5	1,167,882
5	Oscar (by Sadler's Wells)	94	658	14.3	925,521
6	Cloudings (by Sadler's Wells)	29	174	16.7	913,231
7	Beneficial (by Top Ville)	102	756	13.5	897,487
8	Westerner (by Danehill)	56	396	14.1	798,242
9	Flemensfirth (by Alleged)	99	625	15.8	766,125
10	Old Vic (by Sadler's Wells)	54	418	12.9	634,109

LEADING HORSES (1,2,3 earnings)		Races Won	Runs	Stakes £
1	Many Clouds 8 br.g Cloudings–Bobbing Back	4	5	736,648
2	Coneygree 8 b.g Karinga Bay–Plaid Maid	4	4	401,931
3	Dodging Bullets 7 b.g Dubawi–Nova Cyngi	3	4	362,578
4	Faugheen 7 b.g Germany–Miss Pickering	3	3	335,661
5	Silviniaco Conti 9 ch.g Dom Alco–Gazelle Lulu	3	5	311,178
6	Saint Are 9 b.g Network–Fortanea	1	5	240,866
7	Cole Harden 6 b.g Westerner–Nosie Betty	2	6	228,278
8	Uxizandre 7 ch.g Fragrant Mix–Jolisandre	2	4	218,403
9	The New One 7 b.g King's Theatre–Thuringe	4	5	192,886
10	Saphir du Rheu 6 gr.g Al Namix–Dona du Rheu	3	6	161,585

REFERENCE & INDEX

SECTION 5

THE TIMEFORM TOP 100	116
PROMISING HORSES	118
TRAINERS FOR COURSES	120
INDEX	135

HORSES TO FOLLOW
THE TIMEFORM TOP 100

Hurdlers

Rating	Horse
171+	Faugheen
170	More of That
168p	Douvan
168	Arctic Fire
168	Jezki
168	My Tent Or Yours
167	Hurricane Fly
166	The New One
164	Cole Harden
164	Dedigout
163	Whisper
162	Annie Power
162	Un Temps Pour Tout
161P	Peace And Co
161	Saphir du Rheu
161	Thousand Stars
160	Purple Bay
160	Top Notch
159p	Cyrus Darius
159+	Briar Hill
159	Reve de Sivola
159	Rock On Ruby
159	Volnay de Thaix
159	Zarkandar
158	L'Ami Serge
157	Ballynagour
157	Bertimont
157	Shaneshill
157x	At Fishers Cross
156p	Nichols Canyon
156	Abbyssial
156	Kitten Rock
156§	Zaidpour
155p	Vautour
155	Blue Heron
155	Kilcooley
155	Martello Tower
155	Outlander
154p	Thistlecrack
154p	Windsor Park
154	Hargam
154	Henryville
154	Killultagh Vic
154	Milsean
154	Seeyouatmidnight
154	Silsol
153	Medinas
153	No More Heroes
153	Sizing John
152	Activial
152	Arbre de Vie
152	Camping Ground
152	Irving
152	Lieutenant Colonel
152	Val de Ferbet
152	Vaniteux
152	Vyta du Roc
151	Apache Stronghold
151	Bayan
151	Garde La Victoire
151	Jetson
151	Sign of A Victory
151	Wicklow Brave
151	Zamdy Man
150P	Minella Rocco
150	Cheltenian
150	Glens Melody
150	Monksland
150	Noble Endeavor
150	Parlour Games
149p	Aux Ptits Soins
149	Aubusson
149	Bear's Affair
149	Bitofapuzzle
149	Call The Cops
149	Closing Ceremony
149	Gitane du Berlais
149	Rebel Fitz
149	Snow Falcon
149	Taglietelle
149	Zabana
148	Aqalim
148	Polly Peachum
147	Alpha des Obeaux
147	Black Hercules
147	Blaklion
147	Blue Fashion
147	Caracci Apache
147	Deep Trouble
147	Ordo Ab Chao
147	Southfield Vic
147	The Game Changer
147	Theinval
147	Tiger Roll
146p	Kilcrea Vale
146p	Maximiser
146	Dawalan
146	Days of Heaven
146	Glingerburn
146	Hawk High
146	Jollyallan
146	Tea For Two
146	Ted Veale
146	Thomas Brown
146	Value At Risk

Chasers

Rating	Horse
180	Don Cossack
172	Silviniaco Conti
171p	Vautour
170p	Coneygree
170	Djakadam
169p	Un de Sceaux
169	Menorah
168	Dodging Bullets
168	Many Clouds
168	Sire de Grugy
168	Uxizandre
167	Dynaste
167	Road To Riches
167	Special Tiara
166	Al Ferof
166	Balder Succes
165	Champagne Fever
165	Somersby
164	Ballynagour
163	Holywell
163	Sprinter Sacre
162	Cue Card
162	Houblon des Obeaux
162	Sizing Europe
162§	Wishfull Thinking
161p	Don Poli
161p	Saphir du Rheu
161	Carlingford Lough
161	Eduard
161	Mallowney
161	Twinlight
161	Valdez
161§	Hinterland
161§	On His Own
160	Foxrock
160	Mr Mole
160	Rajdhani Express
160	Rocky Creek
159	Boston Bob
159	Felix Yonger
159	Sam Winner
158p	Shutthefrontdoor
158	Johns Spirit
158	Wonderful Charm
157	Baily Green
157	God's Own
157	Roi du Mee
157	Simply Ned
157	The Druids Nephew
157	Unioniste
156	Double Ross
156	First Lieutenant
156	Fox Appeal
156	Lord Windermere
156	Oscar Whisky
156§	Third Intention
155p	Sizing Granite
155	Ballycasey
155	Black Thunder
155	Ma Filleule
155	Smad Place
155	Sound Investment
155	Taquin du Seuil
155	Texas Jack
155	The Giant Bolster
155	Valseur Lido
155x	Hidden Cyclone
154	Argocat
154	Realt Mor
154	Rebel Rebellion
154x	Josses Hill
153	Apache Stronghold
153	Bright New Dawn
153	Long Run
153	Moscow Mannon
153x	Turban
152	Clarcam
152	Croco Bay

THE TIMEFORM TOP 100

152	Gilgamboa
152	Medermit
152	Savello
151P	Vroum Vroum Mag
151p	Gallant Oscar
151+	Irish Cavalier
151	Alderwood
151	Buywise
151	Claret Cloak
151	French Opera
151	Irish Saint
151	Morning Assembly
151	Mount Colah
151	Ptit Zig
151	Rolling Aces
151	Vibrato Valtat
151	Wounded Warrior
150p	Traffic Fluide
150	Australia Day
150	Blood Cotil
150	Bobs Worth
150	Court Minstrel
150	Foildubh
150	Grey Gold
150	Next Sensation
150	Puffin Billy
150	Southfield Theatre
150	Spring Heeled
150	Triolo d'Alene
150§	Hey Big Spender

Juvenile Hurdlers

161P	Peace And Co
160	Top Notch
154	Hargam
145p	All Yours
144p	Bristol de Mai
144	Devilment
142	Pain Au Chocolat
142	Starchitect
141	Beltor
140p	Seamour
140	Buiseness Sivola
140	The Saint James
139	Dicosimo
139	Karezak
138p	Monsieur Gibraltar
138	Bivouac
138	Old Guard
138	Petite Parisienne

138	Stars Over The Sea
137	Fiscal Focus
137	Kalkir
136p	Gwencily Berbas
136p	Intense Tango
136	Bidourey
136	Golden Doyen
135	Bouvreuil
135	Qualando
134	Lil Rockerfeller
133p	Winner Massagot
133	Prussian Eagle
133	Thunder Zone

Novice Hurdlers

168p	Douvan
159p	Cyrus Darius
158	L'Ami Serge
157	Shaneshill
156p	Nichols Canyon
155	Martello Tower
155	Outlander
154p	Thistlecrack
154p	Windsor Park
154	Killultagh Vic
154	Milsean
153	No More Heroes
153	Sizing John
152	Arbre de Vie
152	Vyta du Roc
150P	Minella Rocco
150	Parlour Games
149	Snow Falcon
148	Aqalim
147	Alpha des Obeaux
147	Black Hercules
147	Blaklion
147	Caracci Apache
147	Ordo Ab Chao
147	Southfield Vic
147	Theinval
146p	Maximiser
146	Buiseness Sivola
146	Days of Heaven
146	Glingerburn
146	Jollyallan
146	Thomas Brown
146	Value At Risk

Novice Chasers

171p	Vautour
170p	Coneygree
169p	Un de Sceaux
161p	Don Poli
161p	Saphir du Rheu
157	God's Own
155p	Sizing Granite
155	Valseur Lido
154x	Josses Hill
153	Apache Stronghold
152	Clarcam
152	Gilgamboa
151P	Vroum Vroum Mag
151+	Irish Cavalier
151	Irish Saint
151	Ptit Zig
151	Vibrato Valtat
151	Wounded Warrior
150p	Traffic Fluide
150	Blood Cotil
150	Court Minstrel
150	Puffin Billy
150	Southfield Theatre
149	The Romford Pele
149	The Tullow Tank
148p	Champagne West
148	If In Doubt
148	Oscar Rock
148	Three Kingdoms
148	Virak

NH Flat Horses

126	Bellshill
125p	Yorkhill
124	Shaneshill
123p	Moon Racer
122+	OK Corral
121+	Barters Hill
121	Silver Concorde
121	Value At Risk
120	Definitly Red
120	Modus
119p	See The World
119p	Valerian Bridge
119+	William Henry
119	Lyrical Theatre
119	Urubu d'Irlande
119	Wait For Me

118p	Forgotten Rules
118	Bordini
118	El Namoose
118	Vigil
118	Yanworth
117p	Champers On Ice
117p	First Figaro
117	Anibale Fly
117	Kate Appleby Shoes
117	Princely Conn
117	Pylonthepressure
117	Sheamus
117	Supasundae
116	Beast of Burden
116	Macbride

Hunter Chasers

146	Prince de Beauchene
144	On The Fringe
143x	Twirling Magnet
142	His Excellency
140	Oscar Time
138	Big Fella Thanks
137	Paint The Clouds
137§	Pacha du Polder
136	Baresi
135	Noble Prince
134p	Oscar Barton
133	Aerial
131	Foundry Square
131	Teaforthree
130	Current Event
130	Last Time d'Albain
129	Pearlysteps
128	Carsonstown Boy
128	Neverownup
128	Rockiteer
128	Tataniano
127	Ballytober
127	Hector's Choice
127	Palypso de Creek
127	Seventh Sign
127§	Quinz
125	Following Dreams
125	Rouge Et Blanc
124	Need To Know
124	No Loose Change

* Indicates best performance achieved in a race other than a hunter chase

HORSES TO FOLLOW

PROMISING HORSES

A p symbol is used by Timeform to denote horses we believe are capable of improvement, with a P symbol suggesting a horse is capable of much better form. Below is a list of selected British-trained horses (plus those trained by Willie Mullins) with a p or P, listed under their current trainers.

KIM BAILEY
Ellin's Tower 6 b.m h104p

JIM BEST
New Street (IRE) 4 gr.c h118p
Slowfoot (GER) 7 b.h h128p

MARK BRADSTOCK
Coneygree 8 b.g c170p

DAVID BRIDGWATER
De Kerry Man (IRE) 7 b.g h75 c125p
Gino Trail (IRE) 8 br.g h133p

K. R. BURKE
Intense Tango 4 b.f h136p

MICK CHANNON
Sgt Reckless 8 b.g h142 c133p

REBECCA CURTIS
Audacious Plan (IRE) 6 b.g h123 c129p
Bob Keown (IRE) 7 b.g h120 c119p
Definite Outcome (IRE) 6 b.g h118p
Globalisation (IRE) 5 b.g h109p b95
Moral Hazard (IRE) 6 br.g h100p

HENRY DALY
Nordic Nymph 6 b.m h112p
Tara Mist 6 gr.m h119p

DAVID DENNIS
Ballybough Andy (IRE) 6 ch.g h101 c112p
Final Nudge (IRE) 6 b.g h117p b102

DAVID DUNSDON
Utopian (FR) 7 ch.g c122p

TIM EASTERBY
Chivers (IRE) 4 b.g h100p
Silvery Moon (IRE) 8 gr.g h109p

BRIAN ELLISON
Seamour (IRE) 4 b.g h140p
Zaidiyn (FR) 5 b.g h124p

JOHN FERGUSON
Arabic History (IRE) 5 b.g h113p b111
Chesterfield (IRE) 5 ch.g h139p
Hawker 5 ch.g h108p
Invisible Hunter (USA) 6 ch.g h100p
Ruacana 6 b.g h142 c117p

TIM FITZGERALD
Captain Chaos (IRE) 4 ch.g b106p

JIMMY FROST
Union Saint (FR) 7 b.g h123 c127p

HARRY FRY
Gunner Fifteen (IRE) 7 b.g h124p

Highland Retreat 8 b.m c141p
Mick Jazz (FR) 4 b.g h130p
Zulu Oscar 8 b.g h112p

TOM GEORGE
A Good Skin (IRE) 6 b.g h119 c139p b99
Dexcite (FR) 4 b. or br.g h118p
Just Before Dawn (IRE) 6 b.g b105p

WARREN GREATREX
Aloomomo (FR) 5 b.g h94 c109p
Horsted Valley 5 b.g h107p
Ma du Fou (FR) 5 b. or br.g h115p
Tsar Alexandre (FR) 8 b.g h124 c120p

NICKY HENDERSON
Aigle de La See (FR) 5 gr.g h123 c111p
Beat That (IRE) 7 b.g h143p
Birch Hill (IRE) 5 b.g h118 b97p
Broxbourne (IRE) 6 b.m h131p
Carnival Flag (FR) 5 ch.m h107p b92
Champagne Express 5 b.g h127p
Clean Sheet (IRE) 6 b.g h139P
Coole Charmer (IRE) 6 ch.g b103p
Cup Final (IRE) 6 ch.g h132p
Different Gravey (IRE) 5 b.g h142p
Gaitway 5 b.g h133p
Hunters Hoof (IRE) 6 b.g h125p
In Fairness (IRE) 6 b.g h118p c125
Lessons In Milan (IRE) 7 b.g h135p
Maestro Royal 6 b.g h128p
Might Bite (IRE) 6 b.g h129p b92p
Out Sam 6 b.g h141p
Peace And Co (FR) 4 b.g h161P
Robins Reef (IRE) 5 br.m b104p
Saint Charles (FR) 5 b.g h135p
Sugar Baron (IRE) 5 b.g h129 b112p
Whisper (FR) 7 b.g h163 c137p

MARTIN HILL
Ocean Venture (IRE) 7 ch.g h119p
Tzora 10 b.g h138 c132p

PHILIP HOBBS
Aston Cantlow 7 b.g h110p
Catherines Well 6 b.m h108p
Champagne West (IRE) 7 b.g c148p
Cheltenian (FR) 9 b.g h150 c128p
Drumlee Sunset (IRE) 5 br.g b108p
Georgie Lad (IRE) 7 b.g h111 c117p
Onefitzall (IRE) 5 b.g b107p
Sandygate (IRE) 5 b.g h104p b90
Scoop The Pot (IRE) 5 b.g h117p
Stilletto (IRE) 6 b.g h122p
Sykes (IRE) 6 b.g h118p

The Skyfarmer 7 br.g c132p
Trickaway (IRE) 7 b.g h98p c124

MALCOLM JEFFERSON
Cyrus Darius 6 b.g h159p b90
Urban Hymn (FR) 7 b.g c135p

ALAN KING
Board of Trade 4 ch.g b105p
Bulfin Island (IRE) 6 b.g h109p
Inner Drive (IRE) 7 b.g h132p
Ned Stark (IRE) 7 b.g c140p
Presenting Lisa (IRE) 6 b.m h94 b107p
Roberto Pegasus (USA) 9 b. or br.g h117 c129p
Winner Massagot (IRE) 4 ch.g h133p

EMMA LAVELLE
Casino Markets (IRE) 7 b.g h114p
Javert (IRE) 6 b.g h111p
Private Malone (IRE) 6 b.g h136p
See The World 5 b.g b119p
Set List (IRE) 6 b.g h106p

SOPHIE LEECH
Man of Plenty 6 ch.g h110p

CHARLIE LONGSDON
Battle Born 6 b.g h126p

CHARLIE MANN
Big Jer 8 b.g c113p

DONALD MCCAIN
Bibi d'Eole (FR) 4 ch.g h94 c108p
Clondaw Kaempfer (IRE) 7 b.g h142 c130p
Degooch (IRE) 6 ch.g h118p c119
Final Pass (IRE) 7 b.g h114p
Hester Flemen (IRE) 7 ch.m h134p b112
Keeneland (IRE) 8 b.g c106p
Monbeg Dolly (IRE) 5 ch.m h104p b83
The Last Samuri (IRE) 7 ch.g h130 c137p
Westend Star (IRE) 6 b.g h104p

GRAEME MCPHERSON
Timesishard (IRE) 8 b.g c125p

GARY MOORE
Kingdom (IRE) 5 b.g h102p
Oh So Fruity 5 b.g h101p b92
Remind Me Later (IRE) 6 b.g h124p
Traffic Fluide (FR) 5 b.g h100 c150p

NEIL MULHOLLAND
Fingerontheswitch (IRE) 5 b.g b106p
Minella Present (IRE) 6 b.g h130 c124p

W. P. MULLINS, IRELAND
Clondaw Court (IRE) 8 br.g h136p
Digeanta (IRE) 8 b.g h127p

PROMISING HORSES

Don Poli (IRE) 6 b.g h141p	c161p
Douvan (FR) 5 b.g	h168p
Lockstockandbarrel (IRE) 6 b.g	h121p
Long Dog 5 b.g	h135p
Morning Run (IRE) 6 b.m	h145p b107p
Most Peculiar (IRE) 6 b.g	h135p b99
Nichols Canyon 5 b.g	h156p
Royal Caviar (IRE) 7 b.g	h122p b102
Simenon (IRE) 8 b.g	h141p
Totally Dominant (USA) 6 b.g	h123p b108
Un Atout (FR) 7 b.g	c127p
Un de Sceaux (FR) 7 b.g	c169p
Upsie (FR) 7 b.m	h123 c126p
Val de Ferbet (FR) 6 b.g	h152 c144p
Valerian Bridge (IRE) 6 b.g	b119p
Vautour (FR) 6 b.g	h155p c171p
Vroum Vroum Mag (FR) 6 b.m	c151P
Yorkhill (IRE) 5 ch.g	b125p

WILLIE MUSSON
Broughtons Warrior 7 b.g h116p

DR RICHARD NEWLAND
Boondooma (IRE) 8 b.g h132 c141p
Rock Gone (IRE) 7 b.g h128p

PAUL NICHOLLS
Abidjan (FR) 5 b.g	h127p b78
All Yours (FR) 4 ch.g	h145p
Arpege d'Alene (FR) 5 gr.g	h142p
Art Mauresque (FR) 5 b.g	c143p
Aux Ptits Soins (FR) 5 gr.g	h149p
It's A Close Call (IRE) 6 br.g	h135p
Katgary (FR) 5 b.g	h136 c107p
Le Mercurey (FR) 5 b.g	h138p
Monsieur Gibraltar (FR) 4 ch.g	h138p
Morito du Berlais (FR) 6 b.g	h134p
Rainy City (IRE) 5 b.g	h100p h142p
Salubrious (IRE) 8 b.g	c112p
Saphir du Rheu (FR) 6 gr.g	h161 c161p
Sirabad (FR) 5 b.g	h134p
The Brock Again 5 ch.g	h123p
The Eaglehaslanded (IRE) 5 b.g	h115p b100
Urubu d'Irlande (FR) 7 b.g	h134p b119
Vide Cave (FR) 6 b.g	h100 c120p

FERGAL O'BRIEN
Perfect Candidate (IRE) 8 b.g h119p c129

JONJO O'NEILL
Auvergnat (FR) 5 b.g	h121p c110
Beg To Differ (IRE) 5 ch.g	h132p
Capard King (IRE) 6 b.g	h127p b86
Catching On (IRE) 7 b.g	h121p c140
Forthefunofit (IRE) 6 b.g	h134p
Fort Worth (IRE) 6 b.g	h115p
Gray Hession (IRE) 6 b.g	c130p
Hedley Lamarr (IRE) 5 b.g	h126p
In The Rough (IRE) 6 b.g	h138p
Mad Jack Mytton (IRE) 5 b.g	h124p
Minella Rocco (IRE) 5 b.g	h150p
Rock N Rhythm (IRE) 5 b.g	h117p b96
Set In My Ways (IRE) 4 b.g	b95P
Shutthefrontdoor (IRE) 8 b. or br.g	c158p
The Saint James (FR) 4 b.g	h140 c135p
Which One Is Which 4 b.f	b98p

DAVID PIPE
Champers On Ice (IRE) 5 gr.g b117p
For 'N' Against (IRE) 6 br.g h104p b101

La Vaticane (FR) 6 gr.m	h132p c118p
Moon Racer (IRE) 6 b.g	b123p
Sadler's Gold (IRE) 5 b.g	h111p
Sail By The Sea (IRE) 7 b.g	c125p

JOHN QUINN
Darling Boyz 4 ch.g h105p
Kilas Girl (IRE) 5 b.m h103p
Scoppio Del Carro 4 b.g h109p

KEITH REVELEY
Ivan Boru (IRE) 7 b.g h115 c92p
Midnight Monty 5 ch.g h105p b68
Spiculas (IRE) 6 ch.g h122p

NICKY RICHARDS
Another Bill (IRE) 5 ch.g b105p
Warriors Tale 6 b.g h132p

LUCINDA RUSSELL
Cobajayisland (IRE) 7 b.g h90p c108
Jack Steel (IRE) 5 b.g h106p b57

OLIVER SHERWOOD
Blameitalonmyroots (IRE) 5 b.m h121p
Robinsson (IRE) 5 b.g h115p b99

DAN SKELTON
Bon Chic (IRE) 6 b.m h127p b90
Long House Hall (IRE) 7 b.g h136p b73
Three Musketeers (IRE) 5 b.g h143p
Virgilio (FR) 6 b.g h133p c104p

MICHAEL SMITH
Mister Spingsprong (IRE) 8 b.g h130 c115p
Starplex 5 b.g h108p b93

SUE SMITH
Blakemount (IRE) 7 br.g c128p
Forward Flight (IRE) 9 b.g c115p
Wakanda (IRE) 6 b.g h117p c140

SUZY SMITH
Fin d'Espere (IRE) 4 b.g b74p
Little Boy Boru (IRE) 7 b.g h123 c117p
Red Devil Star (IRE) 5 b.g h119p b86

JAMIE SNOWDEN
Val de Law (FR) 6 b.g c143p

ROBERT STEPHENS
Quebec 4 b.g h128p

TOM SYMONDS
Kaki de La Pree (FR) 8 b.g c138p

COLIN TIZZARD
Kingscourt Native (IRE) 7 b.g h132p b98
Robinsfirth (IRE) 6 b.g h141p
Thistlecrack 7 b.g h154p b94
Zanstra (IRE) 5 b.g h97p b65

NIGEL TWISTON-DAVIES
Ballykan 5 b.g h119p b94
Bristol de Mai (FR) 4 gr.g h144p
Minella Reception (IRE) 9 b.g h124 c128P

JOHN WADE
Dean's Walk (IRE) 6 b.g h102p b95

ROBERT WALFORD
Astre de La Cour (FR) 5 b. or br.g h140p
Camping Ground (FR) 5 b.g h152 c149p
Castarnie 7 b.g h82p c112p

PAUL WEBBER
Orchard Boy (IRE) 7 b.g h120p

SIMON WEST
Maximiser (IRE) 7 gr.g h146p

EVAN WILLIAMS
Buywise (IRE) 8 b.g h119P c151
John Constable (IRE) 4 b.c h127p
Laser Hawk (IRE) 8 b.g h123p
Pobbles Bay (IRE) 5 b.g h109p

IAN WILLIAMS
Portway Flyer (IRE) 7 br.g c122p
Rossmore's Pride (IRE) 7 br.g h118p

NICK WILLIAMS
Abracadabra Sivola (IRE) 5 b.g h122 c106p
Brise Vendeenne (FR) 4 gr.f h107p
Pinkie Brown (FR) 3 gr.g h113p

VENETIA WILLIAMS
Cloudy Beach (IRE) 8 gr.g h109p
Kap Jazz (FR) 5 b.g h102p b58
Spirit d'Armor (FR) 9 b.g h106 c102p
Yala Enki (FR) 5 b. or br.g h118p c130

HORSES TO FOLLOW

TRAINERS FOR COURSES

The following statistics show the most successful trainers over the past five seasons at each of the courses that stage National Hunt racing in England, Scotland and Wales. Impact Value is expressed as a factor of a trainer's number of winners compared to those expected to occur by chance. Market Value is expressed as the factor by which the % chance of an Industry Starting Price exceeds random, as implied by field size. For example, a horse that is shorter than 3/1 in a 4-runner field will have a Market Value above 1.

AINTREE

Trainer	Wins	Runs	Strike Rate	% Rivals Beaten	P/L	Run To Form %	Impact Value	Market Value
Nicky Henderson	35	188	18.62%	55.69	£5.52	26.23	2.06	1.74
Paul Nicholls	20	172	11.63%	55.06	-£37.62	19.94	1.29	1.81
Peter Bowen	18	134	13.43%	53.77	-£21.00	22.85	1.38	1.34
Philip Hobbs	15	106	14.15%	55.44	-£3.00	23.9	1.76	1.62
Nigel Twiston-Davies	13	110	11.82%	56.86	-£21.68	26	1.43	1.44
Donald McCain	12	175	6.86%	46.83	-£104.92	16.2	0.75	1.26
Alan King	11	100	11.00%	55.16	-£20.55	28.37	1.14	1.69
Rebecca Curtis	9	48	18.75%	59.55	-£9.88	22.92	1.93	1.53
Jonjo O'Neill	8	99	8.08%	49.51	-£71.83	15.29	0.93	1.44
Tim Vaughan	7	52	13.46%	50.58	£18.56	25	1.38	1.09

ASCOT

Trainer	Wins	Runs	Strike Rate	% Rivals Beaten	P/L	Run To Form %	Impact Value	Market Value
Nicky Henderson	37	161	22.98%	61.58	-£55.64	35.33	1.85	2.21
Paul Nicholls	34	142	23.94%	62.09	-£6.98	40.85	1.79	1.71
Philip Hobbs	15	94	15.96%	61.81	-£25.55	31.69	1.37	1.38
David Pipe	14	81	17.28%	56.3	-£3.89	27.43	1.73	1.53
Alan King	13	98	13.27%	60.07	£25.38	27.83	1.19	1.28
Venetia Williams	9	70	12.86%	53.2	£2.50	30.42	1.14	1.21
Colin Tizzard	7	44	15.91%	54.13	£5.21	34.09	1.26	1.01
Oliver Sherwood	6	30	20.00%	57.17	-£5.68	45.71	1.69	1.38
Harry Fry	5	11	45.45%	72.16	£6.60	54.55	4.14	1.7
Kim Bailey	5	27	18.52%	52.98	£14.13	29.63	1.67	1.05

TRAINERS FOR COURSES

AYR

Trainer	Wins	Runs	Strike Rate	% Rivals Beaten	P/L	Run To Form %	Impact Value	Market Value
Lucinda Russell	33	286	11.54%	52.8	-£154.88	25.06	0.87	1.14
Donald McCain	31	126	24.60%	54.83	-£12.20	31.67	1.7	1.96
Nicky Richards	27	127	21.26%	56.45	-£19.05	34.41	1.71	1.54
Jim Goldie	26	182	14.29%	50.92	-£14.96	25.64	1.16	1.09
Stuart Crawford, Ireland	12	82	14.63%	59.67	-£6.51	27.98	1.16	1.18
James Ewart	12	93	12.90%	49.39	-£22.28	22.19	1.03	1.02
Paul Nicholls	10	31	32.26%	61.11	£20.68	45.16	2.86	1.92
J. J. Lambe, Ireland	9	49	18.37%	53.22	£18.25	24.49	1.52	0.97
N. W. Alexander	9	114	7.89%	47.24	-£32.25	24.77	0.62	0.89
Nicky Henderson	7	39	17.95%	53.66	-£9.60	30.77	1.72	2.46

BANGOR-ON-DEE

Trainer	Wins	Runs	Strike Rate	% Rivals Beaten	P/L	Run To Form %	Impact Value	Market Value
Donald McCain	75	356	21.07%	56.78	£22.41	30.98	1.46	1.53
Rebecca Curtis	22	78	28.21%	64.14	-£2.85	41.58	1.94	1.99
Jonjo O'Neill	21	182	11.54%	51.58	-£84.75	21.99	0.92	1.44
Charlie Longsdon	18	74	24.32%	59.31	-£10.36	31.94	1.82	1.67
Nicky Henderson	17	64	26.56%	59.83	-£15.94	39.67	1.95	2.64
Venetia Williams	13	98	13.27%	51.34	-£13.34	24.83	1.05	1.13
Philip Hobbs	13	57	22.81%	65.18	£13.12	38.6	1.88	1.69
Nigel Twiston-Davies	10	69	14.49%	58.61	-£11.63	31.19	1.18	1.41
Alan King	10	67	14.93%	57.38	-£16.24	29.03	1.24	1.47
Tim Vaughan	9	70	12.86%	54.44	-£11.34	20.57	0.92	1.5

CARLISLE

Trainer	Wins	Runs	Strike Rate	% Rivals Beaten	P/L	Run To Form %	Impact Value	Market Value
Donald McCain	37	198	18.69%	59.07	-£63.25	29.86	1.42	1.9
Lucinda Russell	22	211	10.43%	52.41	-£77.05	23.92	0.84	1.25
Sue Smith	21	134	15.67%	53.48	-£1.57	30.89	1.27	1.24
Nicky Richards	16	72	22.22%	56.93	£15.45	32.96	1.91	1.51
Alan Swinbank	14	63	22.22%	64.78	£12.95	39.68	1.94	1.99
Jonjo O'Neill	11	52	21.15%	61.97	-£14.32	25.57	1.73	1.72
Venetia Williams	9	27	33.33%	56.42	£18.00	33.33	2.78	1.91
Micky Hammond	8	48	16.67%	54.35	-£7.04	27.59	1.44	1.03
Malcolm Jefferson	7	54	12.96%	60.12	-£2.04	26.35	1.17	1.21
John Wade	7	54	12.96%	49.46	£1.44	21.3	1.13	0.94

TRAINERS FOR COURSES

CARTMEL

Trainer	Wins	Runs	Strike Rate	% Rivals Beaten	P/L	Run To Form %	Impact Value	Market Value
Donald McCain	32	123	26.02%	62.82	-£10.81	31.71	1.8	1.85
Dianne Sayer	14	102	13.73%	54.13	-£11.42	21.98	1.16	1.13
James Moffatt	10	104	9.62%	51.95	£6.25	23.36	0.8	1.01
Peter Bowen	9	45	20.00%	66.23	-£2.38	33.78	1.63	1.78
Harriet Graham	9	37	24.32%	47.7	-£0.76	32.26	1.75	1.11
Nigel Twiston-Davies	7	35	20.00%	61.22	-£9.17	27.14	1.4	1.67
Jonjo O'Neill	7	20	35.00%	69.86	£6.80	45	2.55	2.01
Gordon Elliott, Ireland	6	26	23.08%	63.24	-£6.18	51.92	1.84	2.25
Sophie Leech	6	36	16.67%	47.5	-£3.20	27.78	1.34	1.14
John Quinn	6	18	33.33%	75.65	£5.25	46.46	2.47	2.24

CATTERICK BRIDGE

Trainer	Wins	Runs	Strike Rate	% Rivals Beaten	P/L	Run To Form %	Impact Value	Market Value
Donald McCain	30	141	21.28%	57.87	-£40.15	31.94	1.68	2.05
Keith Reveley	21	89	23.60%	62.68	£69.73	33.71	2.33	1.79
Sue Smith	18	99	18.18%	56.48	£39.79	31.53	1.61	1.28
Brian Ellison	12	48	25.00%	65.05	£2.82	34.07	2.1	1.81
Micky Hammond	9	97	9.28%	54.88	-£25.00	23.68	0.86	0.98
John Wade	9	56	16.07%	53.73	£0.79	34.15	1.5	1.06
John Ferguson	9	16	56.25%	75.6	£10.26	64.29	4.65	3.63
Jonjo O'Neill	6	25	24.00%	56.6	-£3.84	40	1.59	1.79
Michael Easterby	6	35	17.14%	49.3	£10.50	17.14	1.58	1.06
Malcolm Jefferson	6	39	15.38%	54.58	-£2.90	30.77	1.6	1.28

CHELTENHAM

Trainer	Wins	Runs	Strike Rate	% Rivals Beaten	P/L	Run To Form %	Impact Value	Market Value
Paul Nicholls	65	448	14.51%	56.48	-£49.61	31.96	1.49	1.79
Nicky Henderson	53	400	13.25%	58.66	-£101.13	29.95	1.64	1.81
Philip Hobbs	41	286	14.34%	58.37	-£43.34	29.15	1.66	1.47
David Pipe	34	304	11.18%	52.96	-£0.88	24.35	1.47	1.54
W. P. Mullins, Ireland	28	211	13.27%	58.04	-£31.52	29.49	1.88	1.96
Nigel Twiston-Davies	26	300	8.67%	50.06	-£125.15	22.96	0.92	1.17
Jonjo O'Neill	22	181	12.15%	48.58	£9.38	22.65	1.59	1.42
Alan King	17	201	8.46%	55.98	-£23.63	30.97	1.05	1.33
Gordon Elliott, Ireland	12	101	11.88%	56.41	£14.25	38.61	1.57	1.53
Colin Tizzard	10	149	6.71%	47.51	-£29.26	22.15	0.73	1.03

TRAINERS FOR COURSES

CHEPSTOW

Trainer	Wins	Runs	Strike Rate	% Rivals Beaten	P/L	Run To Form %	Impact Value	Market Value
Philip Hobbs	30	151	19.87%	67.17	-£2.87	35.24	1.93	1.82
Paul Nicholls	28	158	17.72%	63.42	-£75.22	28.41	1.63	2.6
David Pipe	27	106	25.47%	63.13	£37.04	39.26	2.65	2.03
Evan Williams	17	141	12.06%	53.06	-£16.88	21.3	1.08	1.13
Peter Bowen	16	86	18.60%	54.64	£32.80	30.2	1.86	1.16
Rebecca Curtis	16	94	17.02%	60.67	-£42.41	31.4	1.45	1.94
Jonjo O'Neill	14	116	12.07%	52.25	-£35.96	22.79	1.27	1.44
Nigel Twiston-Davies	13	115	11.30%	55.14	-£8.07	23.34	1.16	1.28
Victor Dartnall	12	73	16.44%	52.52	£5.38	29.22	1.57	1.36
Venetia Williams	12	118	10.17%	53.76	-£42.88	22.8	0.97	1.25

DONCASTER

Trainer	Wins	Runs	Strike Rate	% Rivals Beaten	P/L	Run To Form %	Impact Value	Market Value
Nicky Henderson	38	107	35.51%	70.01	£41.56	54.4	3	2.68
Keith Reveley	17	113	15.04%	61.56	£6.55	37.56	1.35	1.21
Paul Nicholls	13	59	22.03%	58.36	-£24.58	36.47	1.55	1.96
John Quinn	11	31	35.48%	68.47	£47.25	48.39	2.88	1.6
Alan King	10	94	10.64%	56.91	-£46.84	28.31	0.91	1.82
Emma Lavelle	9	32	28.13%	62.33	£6.83	34.37	2.63	1.86
John Ferguson	9	30	30.00%	67.74	£3.90	44.69	2.62	3.35
James Ewart	8	34	23.53%	62.06	£10.50	39.64	1.82	1.2
Donald McCain	8	79	10.13%	53.84	-£39.13	32.91	0.81	1.42
Philip Hobbs	6	34	17.65%	57.65	£14.75	40	1.44	1.6

EXETER

Trainer	Wins	Runs	Strike Rate	% Rivals Beaten	P/L	Run To Form %	Impact Value	Market Value
Philip Hobbs	43	233	18.45%	57.23	-£53.81	33.78	1.62	1.98
Paul Nicholls	37	141	26.24%	68.62	-£24.44	41.55	2	2.9
David Pipe	32	204	15.69%	55.92	-£61.63	28.6	1.41	1.69
Colin Tizzard	20	136	14.71%	58.63	-£39.92	25.9	1.31	1.32
Victor Dartnall	18	113	15.93%	56.98	£17.00	23.71	1.49	1.28
Susan Gardner	17	115	14.78%	48.88	£22.83	21.74	1.43	0.88
Alan King	16	81	19.75%	63.57	-£5.76	34.21	1.77	1.54
Emma Lavelle	15	95	15.79%	57.09	-£41.17	26.93	1.4	1.75
Jonjo O'Neill	15	108	13.89%	52.01	-£23.05	25.34	1.3	1.42
Jeremy Scott	13	126	10.32%	52.28	-£42.25	24.48	1.03	1.07

TRAINERS FOR COURSES

FAKENHAM

Trainer	Wins	Runs	Strike Rate	% Rivals Beaten	P/L	Run To Form %	Impact Value	Market Value
Gary Moore	43	314	13.69%	52.27	-£36.00	25.51	1.11	1.3
Chris Gordon	41	312	13.14%	51.09	£11.34	23.08	1.04	1
Paul Nicholls	25	79	31.65%	67.51	-£14.57	41.08	1.94	2.36
Tim Vaughan	23	123	18.70%	53.24	-£27.60	24.38	1.38	1.7
Neil Mulholland	21	117	17.95%	53.51	£24.87	27.05	1.42	1.22
Oliver Sherwood	19	73	26.03%	67.04	£55.25	45.05	2.07	1.63
Seamus Mullins	18	162	11.11%	51.12	£42.50	24.96	0.88	1.09
Charlie Longsdon	18	93	19.35%	62.61	-£21.81	39	1.64	1.96
David Pipe	17	77	22.08%	59.69	-£12.24	25.97	1.98	2.06
Nicky Henderson	17	45	37.78%	70.89	£2.34	50.12	2.96	2.55

FFOS LAS

Trainer	Wins	Runs	Strike Rate	% Rivals Beaten	P/L	Run To Form %	Impact Value	Market Value
Evan Williams	64	444	14.41%	49.21	-£9.73	23.06	0.99	1.08
Peter Bowen	58	392	14.80%	54.04	-£110.43	30.06	1.08	1.14
Rebecca Curtis	54	208	25.96%	66.58	£14.44	38.85	1.86	1.93
Tim Vaughan	36	315	11.43%	50.2	-£144.13	21.12	0.82	1.21
Nigel Twiston-Davies	36	192	18.75%	54.78	-£13.94	27.26	1.31	1.39
Jonjo O'Neill	33	176	18.75%	56.59	-£7.35	33.98	1.46	1.65
Nicky Henderson	22	51	43.14%	75.75	-£4.64	50.98	3.16	3.04
David Pipe	22	139	15.83%	56.43	-£35.37	27.51	1.25	1.68
Anthony Honeyball	12	53	22.64%	56.32	£9.96	27.02	1.67	1.61
Bernard Llewellyn	12	125	9.60%	44.97	£42.50	19.86	0.72	0.73

FONTWELL PARK

Trainer	Wins	Runs	Strike Rate	% Rivals Beaten	P/L	Run To Form %	Impact Value	Market Value
Gary Moore	40	269	14.87%	54.42	-£65.47	26	1.24	1.4
Chris Gordon	32	277	11.55%	50.54	£31.51	20.69	0.98	0.93
Paul Nicholls	30	90	33.33%	66.53	-£3.55	43.02	2.17	2.4
Tim Vaughan	22	127	17.32%	53.63	-£47.85	23.99	1.27	1.83
Oliver Sherwood	17	65	26.15%	64.98	£57.75	42.21	2.21	1.52
Alan King	17	74	22.97%	65.88	-£6.29	32.57	1.78	2.08
Jonjo O'Neill	17	86	19.77%	54.74	£6.49	30.53	1.64	1.7
Nicky Henderson	16	37	43.24%	75.89	£5.04	56.76	3.35	2.6
Brendan Powell	15	173	8.67%	50.56	-£75.93	17.37	0.72	1.13
David Pipe	15	87	17.24%	54.75	-£30.49	21.06	1.58	1.97

TRAINERS FOR COURSES

HAYDOCK

Trainer	Wins	Runs	Strike Rate	% Rivals Beaten	P/L	Run To Form %	Impact Value	Market Value
Donald McCain	34	158	21.52%	55.15	-£14.82	35.57	1.66	1.59
Paul Nicholls	14	65	21.54%	62.12	-£1.49	34.39	1.6	1.78
Sue Smith	13	115	11.30%	53.39	£8.25	26.3	0.9	0.99
David Pipe	13	74	17.57%	58.41	£17.71	30.12	2.12	1.55
Nicky Henderson	12	62	19.35%	56.11	-£9.82	26.4	1.6	1.98
Venetia Williams	11	95	11.58%	43.33	-£30.68	18.95	1.06	1.13
Nigel Twiston-Davies	9	83	10.84%	53.67	-£38.89	27.02	0.99	1.23
Alan King	9	59	15.25%	57.92	-£24.56	27.73	1.37	1.29
Lucinda Russell	9	63	14.29%	46.74	£19.50	22.22	1.15	0.9
Evan Williams	8	52	15.38%	53.4	£59.50	30.77	1.38	1.08

HEXHAM

Trainer	Wins	Runs	Strike Rate	% Rivals Beaten	P/L	Run To Form %	Impact Value	Market Value
Lucinda Russell	47	248	18.95%	56.96	-£23.22	28.15	1.49	1.53
Sue Smith	23	149	15.44%	56.96	-£42.83	30.07	1.33	1.34
Donald McCain	20	124	16.13%	56	-£71.87	22.59	1.24	2.14
Ferdy Murphy, France	14	97	14.43%	51.49	£10.38	23.16	1.14	1.14
Stuart Coltherd	12	47	25.53%	56.03	£74.00	37.36	2.11	1.06
Micky Hammond	12	68	17.65%	53.88	-£23.22	27.27	1.52	1.48
Brian Ellison	10	52	19.23%	59.85	-£4.83	28.57	1.42	1.69
Malcolm Jefferson	10	47	21.28%	60.93	-£8.77	31.83	1.79	1.53
George Moore	10	32	31.25%	61.09	£10.12	46.87	2.27	1.48
James Ewart	10	53	18.87%	53.59	£12.38	28.3	1.47	1.32

HUNTINGDON

Trainer	Wins	Runs	Strike Rate	% Rivals Beaten	P/L	Run To Form %	Impact Value	Market Value
Nicky Henderson	38	85	44.71%	78.48	£15.17	52.05	3.88	3.65
Jonjo O'Neill	25	125	20.00%	55.54	-£19.23	27.24	1.83	1.69
Alan King	24	122	19.67%	61.38	-£11.10	33.1	1.7	1.89
Charlie Longsdon	19	109	17.43%	57.02	-£11.06	33.71	1.38	1.58
John Ferguson	19	52	36.54%	75.55	£26.05	50	3.12	2.78
Gary Moore	16	106	15.09%	52.2	£20.71	22.8	1.28	1.27
Venetia Williams	13	80	16.25%	59.49	£52.66	28.57	1.37	1.38
Kim Bailey	13	52	25.00%	62.5	£21.00	42.89	2.16	1.44
Neil King	11	129	8.53%	49.3	£6.25	20.93	0.72	0.85
Ian Williams	10	52	19.23%	56.19	£8.53	23.64	1.59	1.23

TRAINERS FOR COURSES

KELSO

Trainer	Wins	Runs	Strike Rate	% Rivals Beaten	P/L	Run To Form %	Impact Value	Market Value
Donald McCain	39	162	24.07%	61.23	£29.37	36.09	1.85	2.17
Lucinda Russell	31	287	10.80%	52.27	-£90.38	20.31	0.91	1.25
Nicky Richards	26	129	20.16%	56.71	-£0.83	26.21	1.9	1.57
James Ewart	17	110	15.45%	53.9	£12.79	25.67	1.31	1.35
Rose Dobbin	14	127	11.02%	53.64	£6.16	21.63	1.06	1.08
N. W. Alexander	14	138	10.14%	47.01	-£24.05	21.31	0.94	0.97
Chris Grant	13	88	14.77%	58.91	£117.88	30.5	1.37	1.07
Stuart Coltherd	11	88	12.50%	43.12	£43.13	18.24	1.11	0.82
Dianne Sayer	10	116	8.62%	51.84	-£39.00	19.33	0.76	0.97
Malcolm Jefferson	10	64	15.63%	59.29	-£2.70	21.62	1.36	1.57

KEMPTON PARK

Trainer	Wins	Runs	Strike Rate	% Rivals Beaten	P/L	Run To Form %	Impact Value	Market Value
Nicky Henderson	77	241	31.95%	68.1	£87.77	44.18	2.62	2.52
Paul Nicholls	37	182	20.33%	62.61	-£26.44	38.13	1.6	2.04
Alan King	22	188	11.70%	56.7	-£87.64	26.34	1.04	1.62
Philip Hobbs	15	105	14.29%	58.53	-£39.57	25.93	1.26	1.6
Jonjo O'Neill	14	91	15.38%	49.93	-£19.80	23.65	1.56	1.29
Emma Lavelle	14	73	19.18%	54.98	£3.77	32.39	1.69	1.64
Harry Fry	10	26	38.46%	66.93	£62.32	47.96	3.37	1.98
Warren Greatrex	9	65	13.85%	55.05	£0.25	30.77	1.36	1.3
Tom George	9	55	16.36%	53.25	-£7.75	29.09	1.48	1.13
Gary Moore	9	133	6.77%	44.25	-£68.72	15.08	0.62	0.89

LEICESTER

Trainer	Wins	Runs	Strike Rate	% Rivals Beaten	P/L	Run To Form %	Impact Value	Market Value
Nigel Twiston-Davies	15	77	19.48%	57.21	£8.98	33.8	1.52	1.55
Tom George	12	49	24.49%	59.84	£6.85	45.77	1.8	1.61
Venetia Williams	11	48	22.92%	60.71	-£9.00	31.57	1.72	1.76
Nicky Henderson	11	28	39.29%	69.71	£18.72	46.43	2.7	2.2
David Pipe	9	23	39.13%	70.46	£0.12	45.22	3.47	2.6
Tony Carroll	8	68	11.76%	45.08	-£6.00	16.42	0.91	0.81
Neil King	7	31	22.58%	57.96	£3.25	29.03	1.85	1
Caroline Bailey	7	54	12.96%	51.98	-£21.50	27.3	1.01	1
Charlie Longsdon	7	28	25.00%	55.85	£9.10	35.71	1.78	1.18
Jonjo O'Neill	6	52	11.54%	45.23	-£25.20	21.69	0.95	1.09

TRAINERS FOR COURSES

LINGFIELD PARK

Trainer	Wins	Runs	Strike Rate	% Rivals Beaten	P/L	Run To Form %	Impact Value	Market Value
Gary Moore	12	91	13.19%	52.59	-£21.08	21.75	1.01	1.34
Seamus Mullins	7	41	17.07%	50.93	£29.25	23.09	1.29	0.96
Warren Greatrex	7	18	38.89%	70.24	£21.99	38.89	3.15	2.6
Tim Vaughan	6	24	25.00%	54.45	-£0.09	29.17	1.97	1.82
Nigel Twiston-Davies	6	23	26.09%	70.1	£6.37	43.48	1.86	1.71
Nicky Henderson	6	25	24.00%	67.29	-£2.93	56.52	1.81	3.04
Venetia Williams	6	50	12.00%	53.21	£9.38	26	0.88	1.38
David Pipe	5	19	26.32%	65.47	-£2.15	36.84	2.53	2.5
Philip Hobbs	5	10	50.00%	76.55	£2.54	50	3.74	2.29
Charlie Longsdon	5	26	19.23%	56.75	-£14.35	24.26	1.52	2.08

LUDLOW

Trainer	Wins	Runs	Strike Rate	% Rivals Beaten	P/L	Run To Form %	Impact Value	Market Value
Evan Williams	60	307	19.54%	55.5	-£57.38	29.29	1.5	1.43
Nicky Henderson	34	115	29.57%	69.35	-£24.92	40.16	2.56	2.98
Nigel Twiston-Davies	19	163	11.66%	59.1	-£62.77	29.12	1.02	1.44
Philip Hobbs	18	106	16.98%	60.38	-£26.97	29.29	1.56	1.98
Venetia Williams	17	131	12.98%	55.25	-£52.55	22.22	1.14	1.4
Henry Daly	17	132	12.88%	60.59	-£52.90	27.12	1.11	1.36
Rebecca Curtis	13	52	25.00%	67.95	-£10.12	41.67	2.09	2.08
Tom George	11	60	18.33%	57.82	-£2.81	31.36	1.58	1.41
Kim Bailey	11	64	17.19%	65.44	£20.96	40.36	1.57	1.31
Jonjo O'Neill	9	78	11.54%	48.06	-£31.88	22.01	1.15	1.32

MARKET RASEN

Trainer	Wins	Runs	Strike Rate	% Rivals Beaten	P/L	Run To Form %	Impact Value	Market Value
Jonjo O'Neill	36	248	14.52%	53	-£72.01	27.7	1.17	1.52
Charlie Longsdon	33	123	26.83%	61.06	-£11.59	40.35	2.12	1.89
Peter Bowen	26	120	21.67%	60.64	£35.79	36.95	1.99	1.63
Nicky Henderson	26	76	34.21%	67.49	£19.97	44.74	2.83	2.58
Brian Ellison	23	130	17.69%	54.09	£37.44	29.47	1.5	1.3
Malcolm Jefferson	19	122	15.57%	56.01	£23.13	30.61	1.39	1.25
Tim Vaughan	17	146	11.64%	47.14	-£62.27	23.24	0.94	1.34
Steve Gollings	15	92	16.30%	52.7	-£30.74	27.78	1.29	1.54
Chris Bealby	15	93	16.13%	48.36	-£11.72	29.11	1.3	1.01
John Ferguson	15	46	32.61%	73.08	£12.08	43.91	2.87	2.77

TRAINERS FOR COURSES

MUSSELBURGH

Trainer	Wins	Runs	Strike Rate	% Rivals Beaten	P/L	Run To Form %	Impact Value	Market Value
Donald McCain	33	133	24.81%	59.38	£16.40	37.45	1.8	1.78
Lucinda Russell	24	226	10.62%	51.7	-£91.92	22.27	0.82	1.14
Brian Ellison	14	107	13.08%	55.58	-£47.91	27.87	1.09	1.32
James Ewart	11	85	12.94%	53.12	-£41.40	30.79	1.04	1.47
John Ferguson	11	35	31.43%	67.39	£3.79	39.25	2.52	2.49
Jim Goldie	10	114	8.77%	45.54	-£36.75	19.83	0.78	0.92
Nicky Richards	9	50	18.00%	53.44	£16.70	20	1.75	1.67
Dianne Sayer	8	70	11.43%	48.05	£8.75	22.86	0.96	0.78
N. W. Alexander	8	63	12.70%	45.02	-£11.00	23.62	1.07	0.8
Chris Grant	8	76	10.53%	50.35	-£21.00	19.18	0.86	0.91

NEWBURY

Trainer	Wins	Runs	Strike Rate	% Rivals Beaten	P/L	Run To Form %	Impact Value	Market Value
Nicky Henderson	48	239	20.08%	60.37	-£58.20	34.14	1.83	2.2
Paul Nicholls	46	215	21.40%	62.46	-£10.52	37.56	1.76	2.05
Alan King	28	212	13.21%	62.16	-£40.43	34.27	1.25	1.5
David Pipe	22	135	16.30%	57.36	£39.43	28.03	1.63	1.42
Philip Hobbs	21	143	14.69%	56.21	£68.13	30.07	1.43	1.5
Venetia Williams	13	104	12.50%	54.61	-£37.53	27.8	1.09	1.2
Tom George	12	84	14.29%	53.33	-£21.50	33.33	1.25	1.27
Jonjo O'Neill	12	103	11.65%	48.42	-£39.39	24.45	1.19	1.34
Nigel Twiston-Davies	10	107	9.35%	47.06	£1.33	25.23	0.86	1.02
Harry Fry	9	24	37.50%	72.2	£8.92	56.67	2.87	1.98

NEWCASTLE

Trainer	Wins	Runs	Strike Rate	% Rivals Beaten	P/L	Run To Form %	Impact Value	Market Value
Lucinda Russell	30	186	16.13%	55.35	-£7.63	26.38	1.23	1.36
Donald McCain	25	112	22.32%	61.89	£14.70	35.95	1.67	1.93
Keith Reveley	20	104	19.23%	63.09	-£20.45	35.98	1.61	1.73
Sue Smith	14	124	11.29%	54.13	-£41.22	24.4	0.96	1.32
Chris Grant	13	129	10.08%	47.76	-£63.04	19.63	0.86	0.99
N. W. Alexander	12	90	13.33%	47.35	-£4.88	22.72	1.17	1.02
Nicky Richards	12	65	18.46%	55.18	-£9.45	26.26	1.67	1.9
Malcolm Jefferson	11	49	22.45%	65.27	£21.25	38.29	2.02	1.68
John Wade	9	76	11.84%	51.43	-£43.84	28.24	1.03	1.12
Ann Hamilton	8	32	25.00%	62.97	£5.88	56.25	1.64	1.2

TRAINERS FOR COURSES | 129

NEWTON ABBOT

Trainer	Wins	Runs	Strike Rate	% Rivals Beaten	P/L	Run To Form %	Impact Value	Market Value
Paul Nicholls	50	161	31.06%	67.72	£20.18	44.75	2.16	2.22
Evan Williams	31	160	19.38%	59.05	-£20.68	32.71	1.41	1.49
Jonjo O'Neill	28	148	18.92%	49.92	£7.45	26.38	1.65	1.63
Philip Hobbs	26	168	15.48%	60.01	-£22.68	31.44	1.23	1.58
David Pipe	23	207	11.11%	52.37	-£96.73	24.89	1.05	1.51
Tim Vaughan	22	149	14.77%	53.49	-£56.09	25.83	1.24	1.61
Colin Tizzard	17	159	10.69%	54.08	-£46.25	23.05	0.85	1.21
Martin Hill	16	94	17.02%	54.05	£50.38	27.95	1.46	1.11
Nigel Twiston-Davies	16	72	22.22%	56.96	£23.66	30.29	1.71	1.52
Nicky Henderson	15	36	41.67%	73.98	£10.37	55.56	3.55	2.8

PERTH

Trainer	Wins	Runs	Strike Rate	% Rivals Beaten	P/L	Run To Form %	Impact Value	Market Value
Gordon Elliott, Ireland	88	296	29.73%	63.7	£16.59	43.88	2.08	2.2
Lucinda Russell	45	444	10.14%	50.19	-£141.30	23.91	0.75	1.12
Nigel Twiston-Davies	30	116	25.86%	63.21	£30.23	39.92	2.09	1.83
Donald McCain	22	126	17.46%	57.43	-£44.85	28.97	1.16	1.61
Tim Vaughan	19	61	31.15%	67.69	£15.93	44.91	1.85	1.77
Jim Goldie	18	122	14.75%	52.55	-£0.99	25.06	1.12	1.11
Peter Bowen	17	44	38.64%	70.6	£26.63	50	2.79	2.02
Lisa Harrison	14	103	13.59%	53.88	£0.58	30.84	1.12	1
Stuart Crawford, Ireland	14	136	10.29%	53.08	-£60.07	25.19	0.79	1.03
Nicky Richards	13	92	14.13%	56.37	-£2.42	32.2	1.15	1.19

PLUMPTON

Trainer	Wins	Runs	Strike Rate	% Rivals Beaten	P/L	Run To Form %	Impact Value	Market Value
Gary Moore	40	216	18.52%	58.46	-£7.16	29.73	1.39	1.5
Alan King	26	68	38.24%	68.96	£22.59	46.57	2.71	2.18
Seamus Mullins	19	160	11.88%	50.23	-£60.03	22.48	0.85	1.05
Venetia Williams	18	69	26.09%	59.71	-£11.85	32.51	2.01	1.95
Suzy Smith	17	62	27.42%	64.46	£83.63	37.1	2.46	1.14
Chris Gordon	15	139	10.79%	52.01	-£4.00	20.72	0.87	1.17
David Pipe	15	58	25.86%	68.55	£5.25	43.45	2	2.26
David Bridgwater	13	51	25.49%	66.05	£6.28	38.72	1.86	1.46
Charlie Longsdon	13	60	21.67%	54.8	-£9.07	32.77	1.77	1.95
Sheena West	11	79	13.92%	60.58	-£17.67	28.15	1.18	1.16

TRAINERS FOR COURSES

SANDOWN PARK

Trainer	Wins	Runs	Strike Rate	% Rivals Beaten	P/L	Run To Form %	Impact Value	Market Value
Paul Nicholls	39	170	22.94%	63.25	£7.09	37.84	1.78	1.9
Nicky Henderson	38	162	23.46%	60.08	£34.08	35.36	1.98	1.84
Gary Moore	15	115	13.04%	43.5	£13.20	21.89	1.16	0.94
Philip Hobbs	13	90	14.44%	61.14	-£26.10	37.27	1.4	1.6
Alan King	12	80	15.00%	55.62	-£1.17	31.25	1.47	1.48
Venetia Williams	12	95	12.63%	49.62	-£36.93	23.16	1.14	1.19
Charlie Longsdon	10	51	19.61%	57.86	£30.50	27.45	1.94	1.33
David Pipe	7	80	8.75%	49.45	-£46.85	22.73	1	1.5
Nick Williams	6	43	13.95%	56.57	£3.00	32.56	1.27	1.44
Jonjo O'Neill	6	75	8.00%	48.21	-£33.88	12.36	0.8	1.42

SEDGEFIELD

Trainer	Wins	Runs	Strike Rate	% Rivals Beaten	P/L	Run To Form %	Impact Value	Market Value
Donald McCain	64	218	29.36%	64.78	-£20.09	40.94	2.08	2.22
Sue Smith	29	212	13.68%	55.08	-£45.24	27.11	1.08	1.21
Malcolm Jefferson	25	105	23.81%	62.05	£29.79	32.98	1.78	1.31
Brian Ellison	22	109	20.18%	60.54	-£23.07	31.49	1.52	1.85
Dianne Sayer	17	104	16.35%	52.65	-£18.50	26.53	1.34	1.11
Micky Hammond	17	111	15.32%	54.07	£11.50	25.74	1.22	1.06
Chris Grant	17	123	13.82%	49.96	-£29.19	23.35	1.08	0.93
Ferdy Murphy, France	16	122	13.11%	55.26	-£14.00	26.34	1.1	1.12
Keith Reveley	14	61	22.95%	60.36	£22.04	34.94	1.92	1.59
Barry Murtagh	12	72	16.67%	56.18	£32.83	25.39	1.43	1.02

SOUTHWELL

Trainer	Wins	Runs	Strike Rate	% Rivals Beaten	P/L	Run To Form %	Impact Value	Market Value
Jonjo O'Neill	32	172	18.60%	60.54	-£25.34	31.81	1.6	1.85
Charlie Longsdon	22	78	28.21%	61.76	£7.09	37.88	2.22	2.06
Tim Vaughan	18	104	17.31%	58.4	-£18.54	26.2	1.26	1.53
Nicky Henderson	15	61	24.59%	72.03	-£24.60	39.42	1.9	2.96
Peter Bowen	15	72	20.83%	60.28	£17.83	31.05	1.7	1.69
Tom George	15	55	27.27%	64.97	£22.00	42.04	2.27	1.66
Keith Reveley	15	67	22.39%	62.13	£12.46	40.3	1.84	1.59
Caroline Bailey	14	70	20.00%	53.67	£40.71	26	1.49	1.03
Kim Bailey	12	40	30.00%	62.98	£27.48	51.37	2.18	1.72
Donald McCain	11	69	15.94%	53.19	-£32.29	26.47	1.09	1.61

STRATFORD

Trainer	Wins	Runs	Strike Rate	% Rivals Beaten	P/L	Run To Form %	Impact Value	Market Value
Jonjo O'Neill	25	141	17.73%	50.34	£20.44	24.47	1.52	1.44
Tim Vaughan	22	139	15.83%	54.33	-£13.76	26.58	1.33	1.39
Evan Williams	18	120	15.00%	53.55	-£31.48	23.27	1.24	1.37
Warren Greatrex	17	51	33.33%	71.12	£19.87	41.04	2.69	2.16
Philip Hobbs	17	96	17.71%	59.72	-£13.11	29.28	1.48	1.6
Nigel Twiston-Davies	17	122	13.93%	56.56	£34.38	26.89	1.26	1.53
John Ferguson	16	44	36.36%	72	£1.15	47.98	3.13	2.84
Charlie Longsdon	16	75	21.33%	57.15	£13.56	28.6	1.9	1.81
Peter Bowen	15	94	15.96%	62.34	-£23.59	34.98	1.39	1.96
Nicky Henderson	12	62	19.35%	61.82	-£19.54	33.33	1.76	2.39

TAUNTON

Trainer	Wins	Runs	Strike Rate	% Rivals Beaten	P/L	Run To Form %	Impact Value	Market Value
Paul Nicholls	57	182	31.32%	74.84	-£8.55	48.81	2.42	2.73
David Pipe	29	208	13.94%	52.75	-£68.16	27.95	1.33	1.42
Philip Hobbs	21	137	15.33%	60.79	-£55.51	27.22	1.48	1.89
Evan Williams	17	106	16.04%	44.26	£11.01	19.81	1.28	1.18
Venetia Williams	16	86	18.60%	60.18	-£8.60	24.28	1.61	1.7
Colin Tizzard	13	112	11.61%	52.74	-£49.00	23.2	1	1.29
Nicky Henderson	10	51	19.61%	58.48	-£13.67	30.67	1.85	2.79
Alan King	10	92	10.87%	58.3	-£39.73	28.66	1	1.97
Emma Lavelle	9	38	23.68%	65.05	£26.65	41.64	2.07	1.74
Jeremy Scott	9	56	16.07%	62.17	£5.63	33.95	1.6	1.35

TOWCESTER

Trainer	Wins	Runs	Strike Rate	% Rivals Beaten	P/L	Run To Form %	Impact Value	Market Value
Kim Bailey	21	81	25.93%	61.8	£30.74	33.45	2.32	2.06
Nicky Henderson	19	65	29.23%	74.56	-£4.93	37.11	2.71	3.25
Jonjo O'Neill	18	121	14.88%	54.4	-£40.47	23.51	1.44	1.54
Tim Vaughan	16	64	25.00%	58.74	-£6.80	31.25	2.04	1.74
David Pipe	15	55	27.27%	61.29	£4.84	33.21	2.4	2.53
Venetia Williams	15	92	16.30%	61.64	-£45.48	26.68	1.28	1.57
Fergal O'Brien	15	71	21.13%	59.95	£3.55	32.82	1.89	1.62
Nigel Twiston-Davies	15	118	12.71%	53.59	-£38.19	23.28	1.15	1.41
Robin Dickin	14	115	12.17%	51.13	-£44.55	21.15	1.12	1.19
Alan King	14	52	26.92%	74.56	£1.30	41.03	2.44	2.43

UTTOXETER

Trainer	Wins	Runs	Strike Rate	% Rivals Beaten	P/L	Run To Form %	Impact Value	Market Value
Jonjo O'Neill	42	308	13.64%	52.48	-£81.84	24.6	1.23	1.73
Donald McCain	34	262	12.98%	53.38	-£108.40	22.66	1.08	1.6
Tim Vaughan	30	185	16.22%	57.42	-£7.18	27.56	1.33	1.49
David Pipe	29	160	18.13%	57.91	£0.60	25.81	1.7	1.89
Nigel Twiston-Davies	29	152	19.08%	60.17	£8.60	32.14	1.78	1.61
Peter Bowen	22	135	16.30%	56.68	-£37.42	28.77	1.51	1.62
Charlie Longsdon	22	106	20.75%	61.25	-£20.10	36.28	1.95	2.04
Dr Richard Newland	21	68	30.88%	65.46	£12.57	38.46	2.53	2.14
Neil King	21	105	20.00%	59.55	£15.25	31.68	1.65	1.22
Nicky Henderson	17	60	28.33%	67.77	-£4.39	35.98	2.65	2.67

WARWICK

Trainer	Wins	Runs	Strike Rate	% Rivals Beaten	P/L	Run To Form %	Impact Value	Market Value
Alan King	26	116	22.41%	67.53	-£30.83	38.84	1.98	2.16
Nigel Twiston-Davies	18	129	13.95%	52.79	-£6.51	26.85	1.2	1.37
Venetia Williams	17	94	18.09%	56.53	£6.32	28.17	1.58	1.38
Philip Hobbs	15	83	18.07%	60.8	-£19.26	31.32	1.66	1.88
Jonjo O'Neill	13	116	11.21%	52.02	-£29.01	24.52	1.12	1.5
Nicky Henderson	13	43	30.23%	66.48	-£7.23	42.78	2.33	2.67
Paul Nicholls	11	33	33.33%	71.19	£7.51	50.51	2.06	2.18
Charlie Longsdon	11	69	15.94%	59.91	£20.19	33.37	1.41	1.71
Henry Daly	8	69	11.59%	52.69	-£7.25	18.84	1.14	1.22
David Pipe	8	55	14.55%	60.11	-£17.25	30.16	1.45	1.75

WETHERBY

Trainer	Wins	Runs	Strike Rate	% Rivals Beaten	P/L	Run To Form %	Impact Value	Market Value
Sue Smith	29	228	12.72%	50.72	-£82.35	25.08	1.09	1.2
Donald McCain	28	164	17.07%	51.44	-£49.12	27.32	1.32	1.7
Brian Ellison	22	120	18.33%	60.56	-£2.00	30.83	1.65	1.6
Jonjo O'Neill	20	82	24.39%	65.17	-£4.26	37.8	1.96	2
Malcolm Jefferson	14	93	15.05%	56.12	£15.68	26.62	1.32	1.39
Tim Easterby	12	109	11.01%	52.98	-£24.52	25.78	1.03	1.24
Lucinda Russell	12	111	10.81%	49.48	-£21.00	21.21	0.91	1.27
Warren Greatrex	12	27	44.44%	74.28	£32.48	56.41	3.78	2.71
Charlie Longsdon	12	47	25.53%	63.15	-£0.29	34.04	2.36	2.14
Micky Hammond	11	169	6.51%	47.08	-£87.58	16.74	0.61	0.93

WINCANTON

Trainer	Wins	Runs	Strike Rate	% Rivals Beaten	P/L	Run To Form %	Impact Value	Market Value
Paul Nicholls	71	259	27.41%	66.58	-£26.14	43.23	2.1	2.39
David Pipe	34	191	17.80%	55.27	-£29.73	30.33	1.69	1.74
Colin Tizzard	28	199	14.07%	51.32	-£36.17	22.43	1.22	1.31
Philip Hobbs	24	179	13.41%	53.94	-£48.13	25.46	1.15	1.58
Alan King	17	107	15.89%	63.07	-£23.50	30.01	1.36	1.87
Harry Fry	15	55	27.27%	73.7	£16.50	51.71	2.58	2.22
Tom George	13	60	21.67%	62.38	-£12.47	34.39	1.65	1.45
Emma Lavelle	12	67	17.91%	60.92	£23.33	30.62	1.6	1.57
Venetia Williams	12	104	11.54%	55.77	-£39.40	31.69	0.9	1.38
Jeremy Scott	12	104	11.54%	54.36	-£20.88	20.14	0.96	1.15

WORCESTER

Trainer	Wins	Runs	Strike Rate	% Rivals Beaten	P/L	Run To Form %	Impact Value	Market Value
Jonjo O'Neill	63	312	20.19%	57.33	-£15.81	29.74	1.78	1.78
Tim Vaughan	25	171	14.62%	57.31	-£30.95	28.05	1.27	1.52
Paul Nicholls	25	76	32.89%	73.92	£6.43	47.37	2.45	2.58
David Pipe	23	172	13.37%	54.07	-£82.81	19.41	1.16	1.72
Donald McCain	21	120	17.50%	58.93	£8.81	29.89	1.39	1.51
Philip Hobbs	19	107	17.76%	63.71	-£17.07	26.73	1.51	1.83
Nicky Henderson	19	70	27.14%	70.22	-£6.88	38.82	2.39	2.59
Peter Bowen	19	115	16.52%	54.81	-£10.42	33.03	1.49	1.64
Rebecca Curtis	18	63	28.57%	71.58	-£10.57	38.48	2.62	2.63
Nigel Twiston-Davies	17	125	13.60%	53.49	-£29.97	24.59	1.25	1.47

DOWNLOAD THE APP!
Find winners on the move

INDEX

A

Activial	65
Adriana des Mottes	88
A Good Skin (Ire)	4
Aloomomo	65
Altior	61
Alvisio Ville	83
Always Lion	67
Amidon (Fr)	5
Annie Power	74, 110
Apache Stronghold	91, 109
Arbre de Vie	96
Arctic Fire	73, 85, 100, 111, 112
At Fishers Cross	94
Aux Ptits Soins (Fr)	6

B

Ballyhenry	67
Ballynagour	72, 99
Barney Dwan	80
Barters Hill	67
Battle of Shiloh	80
Bay of Freedom	91
Bellshill	91
Beltor	95
Bitofapuzzle	7
Black Hercules	97
Boa Island	60
Board of Trade	8
Boondooma (Ire)	8
Born Survivor	78, 80
Bristol de Mai (Fr)	9

C

Calling des Blins	65
Camping Ground (Fr)	10
Cardinal Walter	101
Carole's Destrier	102
Carraig Mor	102
Champagne Fever	103
Champers On Ice (Ire)	11
Chocca Wocca	12
Clean Sheet (Ire)	13
Cocktails At Dawn	61
Cole Harden	74, 93, 104, 111
Coneygree	71, 75, 97, 107, 109
Copper Kay	14
Corri Lindo	80
Crazyheart	79
Cue Card	103, 105
Cyrus Darius	101, 112

D

Dalia Pour Moi	61
Dawson City	14
De Bene Esse	79

Devilment	95
Dicosimo (Fr)	50
Djakadam	75, 98, 105, 107
Dodging Bullets	74, 88, 109
Don Cossack	72, 75, 92, 103, 105, 107
Don Poli	75, 87, 109
Douvan	73, 82, 112
Douvan (Fr)	50
Drumacoo	67
Duncomplaining (Ire)	15
Dynaste	62, 108

E

Eamon An Cnoic	63
Eduard	93
Empire of Dirt (Ire)	52
En Passe	80

F

Faugheen	62, 73, 85, 111
Fionn Mac Cul,	79
Fletchers Flyer (Ire)	16
Forthefunofit (Ire)	17
Fou Et Sage	64

G

Gallant Oscar	76
Gallant Oscar (Ire)	53
Garde La Victoire (Fr)	18
General Principle	91
Glingerburn	101
God's Own	84
Golden Investment	80
Great Try (Ire)	19
Gunner Fifteen	65

H

Hargam	95, 113
Heathfield (Ire)	54
Herbert Park	62
Hidden Cyclone	93
Holywell	63, 98, 99
Hurricane Fly	85, 106, 111

I

Icing On The Cake	79
If In Doubt	88
Inchiquin All Star	80
Inspired Poet	78, 80
Irish Cavalier (Ire)	20
Irish Saint	92, 102

J

Jessber's Dream	79
Jezki	100, 106, 111

Johns Spirit	64, 93, 103
Jollyallan	83
Jolly's Cracked It	101
Jolly's Cracked It (Fr)	21
Josses Hill	84

K

Kaki de La Pree (Fr)	22
Kings Bandit	63
Kingscourt Native (Ire)	23
Kings Palace	88
Kit Casey	80
Knock House (Ire)	24

L

L'Ami Serge	83
La Vaticane (Fr)	25
Le Mercurey (Fr)	26
Le Reve	76
Lessons In Milan (Ire)	26
Lieutenant Colonel	106
Lucky Pass	78

M

Ma Filleule	92, 99
Many Clouds	63, 76, 98, 108
Martello Tower	96, 113
Medinas	111
Menorah	99, 108
Mia's Storm	79
Mick Jazz (Fr)	27
Milsean	96
Minella Aris	79
Minella Awards	78
Minella Daddy	80
Minella Experience	78
Minella Rocco (Ire)	28
Missed Approach	65
Modus	90
Monbeg Charmer	79
Monbeg Legend	79
Monbeg Rose	78
Monetaire (Fr)	29
Monsieur Gibraltar	60
Montana Belle	90
Montdragon	101
Moon Racer	90
Moon Racer (Ire)	30
More of That	75, 110
Morning Run (Ire)	55
Mr Mole	109
My Tent Or Yours	111

N

Neumond	79
Nichols Canyon	73, 75, 86, 113
No More Heroes	96

INDEX

N (cont.)
No More Heroes (Ire) 55
North Hill Harvey 78

O
OK Corral (Ire) 31
On His Own 98
On The Fringe 76
Our Reward 80
Outlander 87

P
Paint The Clouds 76
Parlour Games 86
Peace And Co 60, 73, 95, 113
Peace And Co (Fr) 32
Petite Parisienne 95
Pleasant Company (Ire) 56
Positively Dylan 79
Pride of Lecale 80
Ptit Zig 92

Q
Qewy 83, 101

R
Red Hanrahan 79
Reve de Sivola 111
Road To Riches 75, 98, 105, 107
Robinesse 63
Rock On Ruby 100
Rolling Dylan 80

S
Saint Are 76
Saphir du Rheu 71, 75, 93, 102, 109, 111
Saphir du Rheu (Fr) 33
Sausalito Sunrise 61
Seamour (Ire) 34
Secret Door 79
Sego Success (Ire) 36

Semper Invicta 79
Shaneshill 82
Shantou Bob 64, 97
Shutthefrontdoor 76
Silviniaco Cont 108
Silviniaco Conti 60, 72, 76, 98, 99
Sire de Grugy 74, 89, 109
Sizing Granite 74, 110
Sizing John 57, 83
Smad Place 99
Smooth Stepper 36
Snow Falcon 87
Some Are Lucky 79
Some Buckle (Ire) 37
Somersby 89, 109
Song of The Night 80
Southfield Theatre 87
Special Tiara 74, 89, 109
Sporting Milan 79
Sprinter Sacre 74, 89, 109
Stowaway Magic 79, 80
Supasundae 90
Sure Reef 62
Sutton Manor 78
Sweetlittlekitty 80

T
Tell Us More 83
The Druids Nephew 76
The Fresh Prince 79
The New One 85, 111
Theo's Charm 90
The Saint James (Fr) 38
Thistlecrack 75
Three Musketeers (Ire) 39
Toowoomba (Ire) 40
Top Notch 73, 95, 113

U
Un de Sceaux 74, 84, 109, 110
Unowhatimeanharry 41
Unravelthemystery 79
Un Temps Pour Tout 94, 104, 111

Urano 62
Uxizandre 74, 92, 107

V
Vago Collonges 101
Valseur Lido 75, 91, 109
Value At Risk 42, 64
Vautour 75, 91, 109
Vibrato Valtat 84
Vigil 90
Virgilio (Fr) 42
Volnay de Thaix 100
Volnay de Thaix (Fr) 43
Vroum Vroum Mag 110
Vukovar 99
Vyta du Roc 86

W
Wait for Me 61
Wait For Me 90
Wait For Me (Fr) 44
Wakanda 102
Welsh Shadow (Ire) 45
Whatswrongwithyou 79
Which One Is Which 46, 64
Whisper 74, 94, 104, 111
William Henry (Ire) 46
Windsor Park 75, 113
Winner Massagot (Fr) 47
Wounded Warrior 75, 87

Y
Yanworth 90
Yorkhill (Ire) 58
You Say What 80

Z
Zabana 106
Zarib 64
Zarkandar 94, 104, 111
Zeroeshadesofgrey (Ire) 48

Index To Photographs

	Photographer	Page
Aux Ptits Soins lands the Coral Cup at Cheltenham on his British debut	John Crofts	6
The well-regarded grey Champers On Ice (carrying Bryan Drew's colours) makes a winning debut at Punchestown	Caroline Norris	11
Garde La Victoire leads over the last in the Greatwood Hurdle	Bill Selwyn	18
Jolly's Cracked It looks a fine chasing prospect	Ed Byrne	21
Champion Bumper winner Moon Racer is expected to take equally high rank as a novice hurdler	Caroline Norris	31
An impressive success in the Mildmay for Saphir du Rheu	Ed Byrne	34
Three Musketeers is a very exciting hurdling prospect	George Selwyn	39
Wait For Me has the potential to develop into a leading novice hurdler this season	Bill Selwyn	45
Douvan looks another star for Willie Mullins	George Selwyn	51
Gallant Oscar is a staying chaser to follow in handicaps	Caroline Norris	53
Ben Pauling	Bill Selwyn	66
Dual Betfair Chaser and King George winner Silviniaco Conti	Alec Russell	72
Peace And Co (left) challenges stablemate Top Notch at the last in the Triumph Hurdle	Peter Mooney	73
Don Cossack leads over the last in the Punchestown Gold Cup	Caroline Norris	108
The imperious Un de Sceaux	Caroline Norris	110
The unbeaten Faugheen leads home his stablemates Arctic Fire and Hurricane Fly (hidden) in the Champion Hurdle	Ed Byrne	112